Build-A-Book Geometry

A story of student discovery

By Christopher C. Healy

KEY CURRICULUM PRESS
Innovators in Mathematics Education

Cover art by Bernard Garcia.
Designed by Ann Rothenbuhler.

Printed in the United States of America

ISBN 1-55953-066-9

Foreword

Near or at the top of any list of objectives for education that I have ever seen is the goal of having students assume authority and responsibility for their own lives. One can argue about how well, over a long period of time, we attain this goal. One thing is certain. We do not do as well as we might, as evidenced by the anomie, disengagement, and frustration that characterize the lives of many of our adolescents.

Many forces play a role in shaping our society at all levels. It would be foolish to isolate any single influence on any single part of society and claim that changing it, by itself, could produce large-scale, systematic societal change. Nonetheless, we all probably believe that this world would change for the better if we could get students to assume more authority and responsibility for their own lives.

If we choose to address this goal, we must ask ourselves what we can do, as educators and parents, to foster its attainment. This book shines light on that question.

Chip Healy is a mathematics teacher in a high school in Los Angeles. He is a man who cares deeply about teenagers and the people they are becoming. His efforts in their behalf go well beyond the mathematics classroom. He coaches track, directs drama, and serves as a student advisor. During the summer he works in a local recreation program, and on weekends he is in charge of the youth program of a local church.

This book is the story of how this man and his students evolved a way of making real the assumption of authority and responsibility in what most people would regard as a most unlikely setting: the mathematics classroom. Healy's notion was that if Euclid could develop geometry thousands of years ago, it is possible that a group of high-school students, with the technology of today, could travel that same road, rediscovering for themselves the extraordinary tapestry of objects and relationships that characterize the subject.

As a result, the students in Mr. Healy's room learned to think independently, to make and explore conjectures, to communicate ideas, to pose and to solve problems, and above all, to collaborate and communicate with others.

The story of the No Book class is told from several perspectives. We see the class through the eyes of its teacher. In addition, Chip has written this story from the perspective of five of his students so that we can see how the class might have looked through their eyes. The intertwined threads of story give us a rich portrait of an experience that left a deep mark on all of those who participated in it.

Suppose that schools were places where young people were regularly asked to participate actively in the making of the knowledge they were asked to acquire—as they were in Chip Healy's room. Could we come to expect, even in some small measure, that youth might become engaged in ways that they otherwise would not have? The evidence is still slim, but it is promising.

"Intellectual Mirrors" are crafted software environments that allow users to explore the depth and breadth of their own understanding. One such environment, *The Geometric Supposer*, written by my colleague and me, played a role of some importance in Chip Healy's No Book class. I like to believe that it contributed in some measure to the remarkable outcome for those involved.

Can we afford a small measure of optimism about schools and schooling as we find more and more Chip Healys and arm them with tools that aid them in fashioning a different kind of school experience for their students? I would like to believe the answer to be yes.

Judah L. Schwartz
Truro, MA

Introduction

I believed strongly that if Euclid could develop geometry, then a class of today's high school students could do the same thing. I just hoped they would cover topics similar to those taught in traditional geometry classes, but there was no assurance. So, in groups of four (which changed randomly every two weeks), the class built their own geometry curriculum. In doing so, they learned a great deal about geometry and what makes geometry work, but they learned more than just geometry. They learned to take responsibility, cooperate, communicate, think critically, and be creative. And they learned about themselves and each other.

Those of us who became math teachers over the past few decades did so for a variety of different reasons. But when we considered teaching mathematics as our future, few were aware of the future direction of mathematics education. Teaching math wasn't difficult: for each problem there was only one right answer, textbooks always included a teacher's edition, and most curriculum plans had their own tests (which were easy to grade). The subject matter might have been a little dry, but it was easy to disseminate to the students who cared to absorb what we taught.

Of course, there were always failures in math, but they were easy to dismiss. It was simple: "Some people can't do math." That statement was readily accepted as an educational reality. Consequently, there was no teacher failure or textbook failure, only a certain segment of the student population who couldn't do math. It was too bad, but the blame was not placed on the math teacher.

The formula for creating math teachers in the past was clear: Take a "can" student with a desire to spend all of his or her working hours in a classroom, and *voilà*—a math teacher was born.

Today we are faced with the conflict between what we thought was a fundamental truth and what we now know to be reality—there are no "can'ts." The words *can* or *can't* must be replaced by *choose to* or *choose not to*. Mathematics is not some deep, dark jungle that can only be explored by a limited percentage of the population with the proper guide (aka teacher). The subject is accessible to anyone who chooses to pursue it, and it must be perceived as such. The job of the teacher is to facilitate this decision and to assist learning. In many cases this is not what math educators expected in the trenches of the mathematical classroom. But it is the future of mathematics education, and teachers of the present and future must adjust to it.

Since the fall of 1987, hundreds of educators have seen mathematics become accessible to students in my Build-A-Book (originally called No Book) geometry class at Mountain View High School. Visitors became involved with the students developing theories, uncovering unknowns, investigating conjectures, and pursuing the impossible. Up to now, a classroom visit was the only way for an outsider to understand why such special things took place in that class. I wrote *Creating Miracles* so more people could experience this class through the eyes of six of the pioneers.

The students were not specially designated; when they entered the class, they were a cross-section of the high school population. But by the time they left, they were empowered in a way that no one could have predicted. The command of mathematics and of themselves that came as a result of this first No Book class prompted me to offer at least one class each year. It is my hope that others reading about the Build-A-Book class will be inspired to take risks and discover similar benefits for themselves and their students.

Taking risks with the curriculum was probably not what most of us expected when we made the decision to become professional educators. However, in the future, daring to try new things will become an integral part of our profession.

Teaching mathematics has been comfortable for the most part, but with risk taking it may become uncomfortable. No matter how uncomfortable risk taking makes us feel, it is necessary if we are going to prepare our students for the unknown, unpredictable world that lies ahead of them.

Developing the skills for taking risks takes the one thing most of us don't have—time. That time came for me at an institute called MSTI (the Math/Science Technological Institute, pronounced "misty"). MSTI was a four-week, live-in experience for two hundred teachers that removed me from the demands of home life, exposed me to the latest technology and software, and allowed me free time. The unstructured hours gave all of us time to relax, think, network with colleagues, and consider alternatives.

I am a strong advocate of that type of experience for all teachers. MSTI reaffirmed my confidence in myself and was fundamental in my taking the risk of developing the Build-A-Book class. Taking risks is not natural for me or anyone, but it can be the most stimulating thing a teacher does during his or her career.

While I was at MSTI I asked myself some significant questions that led to my risk taking. I believe all teachers ought to take a few minutes alone to ask themselves these questions. The questions and their answers helped me discover my own optimum teaching environment and gave me the courage to take the risk of Build-A-Book. In order for the questions to be useful, though, the answers need to be honest and must not be influenced by outside sources. They need to be internal answers.

These are the questions I asked myself while I was at MSTI, along with my own internal answers:

1. *Why did I choose to become a teacher?*
   a. A promise I made to one of my college professors.
   b. I have always enjoyed young people.
   c. I didn't know what else to do.
2. *What are my favorite parts of teaching?*
   a. The things that happen outside the classroom.
   b. Helping kids create their lives and become successful.
3. *What are my least favorite parts of teaching?*
   a. Paperwork, textbooks, and discipline.
   b. Kids who don't care about themselves.
4. *What are my greatest strengths as a person?*
   a. Working with and understanding young people.
   b. A sense of humor.
   c. Belief in myself.
5. *What are my greatest strengths as a secondary math teacher?*
   a. Relating to students and helping them reach their goals.
   b. Motivating students to learn.

c. Creativity in the classroom.

6. *What are my biggest weaknesses as a person?*

   a. Lack of organization.

   b. Aversion to reading or dealing with technical material.

7. *What are my biggest weaknesses as a secondary math teacher?*

   a. With only a minor in math, I feel I lack important knowledge of mathematics.

   b. Lack of time or interest to prepare.

8. *Why am I not thriving where I am?*

   a. I am accomplishing all I can in the classroom, considering all the extracurricular activites in which I am involved.

   b. I choose not to consider change. I know things need improving, but I don't know what to do. I wait for something (someone) else to make things better.

My responses to the questions give an accurate impression of who I was at MSTI. At the time I was unaware of it, but my responses were clues to my optimum teaching environment and to the direction my risk taking would take.

I considered my responses to the questions and what I knew to be true about geometry and decided to take the risk that has resulted in this book. I felt insecure in my mathematical knowledge. I am not very organized. I work better creating things on the spur of the moment than with extensive preparation. I care about kids and their lives inside and out of my classroom. I felt there needed to be a change in the geometry curriculum in my class. Given these characteristics, the Build-A-Book class was a natural. It was consistent with who I am that the concept was an unplanned whim. After teachers have dealt with who they are as individuals, they can consider whims and alternatives that will fit them as teachers.

Taking risks is less fearful when it is clear that the risk one is taking is consistent with one's basic nature. Build-A-Book fit my

It wasn't comfortable, and there were no guarantees, but it fit me and it was the most exciting thing that has happened to me in teaching. It has never become comfortable, even after repeated classes, but it has never been boring either.

In the educational world, Build-A-Book is a unique experience. After three months, one student described the experience like this: "In this class we make enemies out of friends arguing over things we couldn't have cared less about last summer." Clearly, Build-A-Book classes develop students who are passionately concerned about mathematical issues in which they previously had no interest.

By the end of the school year, the students own the information they have created and they have learned to interact positively with each other. They are empowered with mathematics and with understanding that they gained from being given the freedom to think in a positive environment. I wish I could take every teacher into a Build-A-Book class to see what can come of taking risks.

Because it is impossible for everyone to physically visit a Build-A-Book class, I wrote *Build-A-Book Geometry* to simulate a Build-A-Book experience for the reader. I felt the Build-A-Book class couldn't be fully experienced seen just through my eyes, but needed to be seen from students' perspectives. All the people who have visited any BAB class have gotten involved with the students and their enthusiasm for their discoveries—the experience cannot be accurately described without the students' points of view.

For this reason, I've chosen to write parts of this story based on what I imagine the thoughts of these students might have been. (You can read students' own words in Appendix 3, a photo-reproduction of an actual, student-created book.) Over the course of the year I got to know my students very well. I spent many hours talking with them and discussing their projects, the class, and their lives. All of the class incidents described here really happened in Build-A-Book. Most of the incidents in this book that happen outside of class actually happened too. Chris, Larry, Edmund, and Alicia are based on actual, specific students, whereas Carmen is more a composite character. I didn't attempt to change reality, but there are places where I couldn't know exactly what had taken place. In these cases, I wrote entries to clarify points to the reader. (For example, I knew little of Edmund's family background, but what I wrote helps define who Edmund was at the time.) The students upon whom Chris, Larry, Edmund, and Alicia were based have read their chapters and each of them remarked that their chapters were remarkably accurate.

One of my goals with this book is to transport you to a Build-A-Book classroom. If I've succeeded, you will see and feel the enthusiasm on the students' faces, their dogged determination in pursuit of discoveries, and their excitement when they reach a conclusion. I hope that by writing from my student's points of view I've made the book a more "real" simulation of what happens to the students and teacher in a Build-A-Book class.

New software, like *The Geometer's Sketchpad* and *The Geometric Supposer,* makes changes in the geometry curriculum less threatening. The graphing calculator in algebra and improved textbooks and software in pre-algebra will help. Every year more advanced technology and improved books are available to teachers in every subject at every level. But it is up to the individual teacher to take the risk of venturing beyond the comfortable. May your journey through the original No Book geometry class in the following pages empower you to take risks and find your own teaching adventure.

Chapter 1

ès

Three Measly Times
(Christina's thoughts—August 25)*

T his was supposed to be my best summer ever. I had it all planned so that I could spend every day at the beach with my friends in Long Beach, but I only got to go to the beach three measly times the whole vacation. And now summer's almost over—today I had to register for school. When we moved from Long Beach to El Monte a little over a year ago, I couldn't believe it. I was so mad at my father for making us move the way he did, I was sure I would never talk to him again, but of course I did. Even though we lived here my whole sophomore year, most of my best friends are still in Long Beach. But this summer I was going to go back and be with all of them (well, most of them). I know things weren't perfect when we lived there, but I did have a lot of friends and I was just starting to get involved in things at school. And, for the first time since I left sixth grade, my grades were getting better.

*Editor's Note: Author Chip Healy wrote this story based on his experiences with real students. He writes from students' points of view so that we can experience the events from what he imagines the students' perspectives would be. See Appendix 3 for examples of actual student writing.

In the sixth grade my grades were really good and my teachers gave me the award for being the "most likely to become a doctor" (or something like that). My sixth-grade teacher, Miss Salcido, always wore this certain perfume. I can still smell it when I think about it real hard. She really believed in us (especially me, I think). She used to say, "You can do anything you really want to do." I don't know if she's right in my case, but it sure made me feel good to think that someone really felt that way.

The other thing that happened to me that year was Sylvia. She was in my class and she failed practically everything, but she sure was popular. In fact, Sylvia had a *boyfriend*. A sixth-grade boyfriend is nothing big now, but then it was really something. I knew Sylvia liked me because she laughed at my jokes. That's what I did best then—tell jokes. Anyway, the award I got from my teachers was great, but the best thing that happened to me that year was when Sylvia let me hang around with her and her friends.

I spent nearly the whole summer with Sylvia and the other girls. When I started ninth grade the next fall everything was really different. We just talked, looked at guys, had lunch with everyone, ditched classes and stuff. I never knew school could be so much fun. My grades went down, but I didn't care. I finally had some people to hang around with. I even got a boyfriend.

Looking back now, I can't believe I liked Bobby. He treated me like I was nothing, but he was on the eighth-grade football team and he could drink more than anybody I knew; so he went to all the parties, and finally I got to go too. The parties weren't that great because I didn't used to drink. But now I was *at* the party and not just hearing about it the next day from the other girls. I think they always made it sound better than it actually was.

Bobby lasted until football season was over and then he dropped me. All the time Bobby and I were together, there was this David guy at the parties. He was really tall and seemed left out like me, so I ended up talking to him. He was okay, but everyone made fun of him because he was so tall. I didn't want to stick out because everyone would notice that I wasn't drinking, so I talked to David. I felt sorry for David because he didn't drink either. I think it's more important for guys to know how to drink.

All the time I'd been with Bobby I told my parents I'd been going to the library to study. But after report cards came out at the end of the first semester, my parents made me stay home. So when Bobby dropped me, it was okay because I couldn't go to the parties any-way—maybe that's why he dropped me. The rest of the year I just hung around with Sylvia and her friends. We began ditching school and going to the beach instead.

The teachers didn't like to have us around because we didn't do what they wanted. So when we were gone, they were happy and so were we. It made everyone happier. My grades the second semes-ter were even worse than first semester. But the only thing I cared about was not failing. I knew my dad would've killed me if I ever failed a class.

That summer Sylvia went to stay with her aunt in Mexico, so I never saw her, but I saw the rest of the girls. They were always to-gether ... without me. I saw them at the beach or at the movies, but they weren't my friends anymore. It really hurt to know that my only real friend in that crowd had been Sylvia.

That was when I found out that my little sister, Letty, was fun to have around. Mostly she had been just a dumb little kid before then, but somehow that summer she grew up or something. So I spent a lot of time with her. Letty was my new friend, even if she did still do some stupid stuff—like she used to scream every time she thought she saw a shark. And she had such an imagination that she "saw a shark" almost every time she went in the water. At first it was kind of embarrassing, but at least I knew she wanted to be with me and I got used to the shark screams. By the end of the summer, we even used to joke about it.

When school started, Sylvia came back, and so did my "friends." I still did things with them, but it was different.

I guess I got cute or something over the summer, because I had the guys from the eighth-grade football team around all the time. It was great. I went to all the parties that year and didn't even have a boyfriend, I just got invited.

After the football season I was still going to the parties. I could have had my choice of boyfriends. That sounds so conceited, but I think it was true. It's funny, when I could've had my pick, I didn't care.

Then at a Valentine's party, I talked to David, who'd gotten a lot cuter. He told me that I was the only one who would talk to him the year before. Then he thanked me for it—can you believe it? That's when I got interested in him.

I saw David the rest of the year in eighth grade. The funny thing was, after I met David, when I told my dad I was going to the library to study, that's what I did. I spent the time studying with David. He told me he was going to be a pediatrician. That's a doctor for kids, even the kids like the ones that had been mean to him. I decided to try to be something special, too. Maybe not a doctor, but something.

I stopped ditching school and tried to get my grades back up to where they were in the sixth grade. It's hard to change after the teachers think you don't care. I guess I gave them a reason to think I wasn't much of a student, but sometimes people can change. It's not fair when people don't let you change. I think they should have been willing to let me start over. But they didn't, so I ended up with mostly B's. Which wasn't bad, considering the grades I'd had.

Do you know what really made me mad? My dad took all the credit for my grades going up. He said, "I know you studied because you wanted to make me proud of you."

It's true that I want him to be proud of me, but I didn't study for him. He didn't deserve any of the credit. I studied for David... and me, I guess.

I saw David most of that summer. We spent almost all of it at the beach, and you should have seen David in a bathing suit. He was six foot-two and built, I mean *built*. He worked out with weights almost every morning for two hours. And he seemed to get cuter and cuter. And there's this other thing. I know it sounds weird, but he has this kind of way he smiles when he's pleased. He turns his lips up at the corners in this way I can't describe. I always tried to do things that pleased him so I could see that smile.

Like the day I was trying to body surf. I never was much of a swimmer, but I knew if I could learn how to body surf, I'd see that smile from David.

Unfortunately, I got caught in the riptide. I started to get carried away from the shore, and I guess I just panicked. All I remember was David carrying me out of the water. I looked up and saw that smile. Then he said, "Chris, you have to be more careful if you are going to be my girl." His girl! Wow! There I was nearly drowned, feeling better than I'd ever felt before in my life.

When we got back to school in the fall, I spent most of my time studying or going to football practices and games—David played on offense and defense. At the end of the season he was voted Most Valuable Player on the freshman team, and the next year the coaches told him they wanted him to play varsity. Things were going great, except my parents and I weren't getting along. I had lots of new friends, and my grades were nearly straight A's.

Julie, my best friend, and I spent lots of time together because her boyfriend was on the team with David. We were in the same math class, so we went to the football games together and studied algebra together. On Saturdays we went to the beach when our boyfriends had to watch game films. Julie liked my jokes as much as Sylvia ever did, but she even liked me when I wasn't being funny.

One day Julie told me she was going to run for second-semester freshman class president. Then she said, "I think it would sound pretty good: 'Vote Julie for President and Chris for Vice President.' What about it?" I couldn't believe it. I told her I had to think about it.

When the day came to sign up for the election, I thought, "No one will vote for me, but what the heck." Signing up was easy, but saying a speech to the freshman class was one of the hardest things I'd ever done.

After the speeches, everyone voted. That afternoon when they announced the winners, I was so nervous. First secretary, next treasurer, and then the announcer said, "and the new freshman class Vice President is ..." (it seemed like he waited forever) "Christina Delatorre." I won! Not only that, but Julie too. And I knew David would smile that smile when he heard. I didn't see David that day because he had a basketball game at some other school. And I never got to see that smile because of what happened at home.

When I got home, I couldn't wait to tell my parents about the election. I wanted to share my successes with my family, because that's the way I think it should be. First, I sat them both down together and had them hold hands. Then I announced it just like at school.

They never even congratulated me. My dad said that I could only do it if it didn't interfere with my studies, which it wouldn't have. And, I couldn't be vice president if it meant doing anything in the evenings or on weekends. When I told them I had to go to the freshman class meetings on Tuesday nights at school, they said I had to resign.

So, the first thing the next day I went into the office and told our class advisor that I had to resign. I said my parents reminded me I had other obligations. I couldn't tell him the real reason. I didn't want him to think my parents were bad people or anything.

When I saw David I just turned and went the other way as fast as I could. I knew that his special smile (that I'd thought so much about since I won) wouldn't be there. And I was afraid he'd be disappointed in me, which made me feel awful.

From that day on my relationship with David got worse and worse. We had planned to spend Easter vacation together, but I was just too uncomfortable around him. He was so successful and I was sure he thought I was a quitter. So on Good Friday, the day before the vacation, I told David I wanted to break up. He didn't get mad or yell at me or even try to change my mind, he just gave me a kiss and said he understood. It wasn't a "good" Friday and David didn't "understand." I needed him more at that point than at any other, but it just couldn't be. My parents were ruining my life without even trying.

After Easter vacation I talked our advisor into holding the class meetings at lunch, so I wouldn't have to go out at night. I planned on running for office again, and this time my parents couldn't stop me. I even thought about maybe getting back with David. Then my parents told Letty and me that we were going to be moving after school was out. It's almost as if they knew exactly how to ruin my life. I hadn't even let them know about running for office and they had already wrecked my chances.

So in June we moved to El Monte. Mom said we couldn't go back to Long Beach and visit until the next summer. I kept thinking about my old friends and wondering if they were at the beach. At least Letty and I had a good time together, though. Letty laughed at my jokes almost as much as Sylvia or Julie did. I like to make her laugh. She seems like a serious person sometimes, but other times she likes to just joke around. I like those times best.

When summer was over we went to Mountain View High School. Letty was a freshman and I was a sophomore. At the start Letty and I hung around every day, until she started seeing this guy. I got to know a bunch of girls who liked some of the guys on the JV football team. It worked out okay. The guys thought I was smart because I knew so much about football (thanks to David). By Halloween, I had a boyfriend. Raul was fun to be with because he was always joking around. He kind of made me forget about David. Raul wasn't serious about anything.

Raul was the one who taught me how to drink. I didn't like the taste very much and I was worried about becoming an alcoholic, but it didn't seem to matter so much at that point. The problem with Raul was he got carried away when he was drunk. He hit me a few times and yelled at me a lot. Who did he think he was, my father or something? Anyway, it ended on New Year's Eve. Raul expected me to sleep with him to begin the new year and I told him off.

In March, when Little League started, I went to see my little brother's games. To be in Little League here, one of your parents has to volunteer to work for two hours in the snack bar twice a season. I knew my parents wouldn't do that, so I told my brother that I would. The third game of the season I was working in the snack bar and I got home late. When I got there, my dad accused me of all sorts of things and grounded me for a month because of it. Sometimes parents can drive you crazy.

It seems like parents are so worried about what's going to become of their kids that they don't let them become anything. I don't think my parents have any idea what is important to me and how I feel about things. I sure hope I listen to my kids better than my parents listen to me.

So my sophomore year wasn't so great, but I knew that I could spend the summer at the beach with my friends from Long Beach. I wrote to David and told him about it, but he didn't write back. Then I wrote Julie, and she did write back. She said everything would be great. So it was all set up, no problems.

Julie's letter also said that David had a new girlfriend. It's okay, I guess. I mean, I didn't expect him to be a monk or anything. I just thought that maybe this summer David and I could get back together. Well, I hope he's happy ... but not too happy. I can't believe I feel like this. I want him to be happy, but only if it's with me. That's so selfish. Why do I think things like that?

My plans were all set and I was ready for the best summer of my life. Unfortunately, my mother had other plans in mind. Things like washing clothes, cleaning the house, and watching my little brothers. It's not that I'm ungrateful or that I'm not willing to help out, but she promised we could go back to visit Long Beach this summer. I want to help around the house and I love my little brothers, except for times when they try to make a fish mud pie using *my* goldfish and the water in *my* fish tank and cooking the pie on the floor in *my* room. Watching them all summer wasn't what I had in mind, and Mom knew that. Especially this summer—it was going to be a super summer. I think I deserve it because I'm finally going to be an upperclassman, that's better than my mom ever did in school. So I worked for her every day except for three. That's why I know out of the whole summer I went to Long Beach exactly three times. It's just not fair.

I know it's not easy having four kids, especially if two of them are like my brothers. They always seem to be getting into trouble one way or another. It's funny—my parents don't ever get very mad at my brothers; the only time they get really upset is when Letty or I do something that they don't think is "right for a girl our age." What's so special about being a boy?

At least school starts soon so I'll be out of the house. I don't know how well I'll do this year. I've got this counselor who thinks I'm going to college (the poor guy just doesn't understand). I don't want to disappoint him, but two more years of this education stuff and I'm done forever. Then I'm getting a job and moving out.

Anyway, when I registered for school today I took the classes that my counselor wanted me to. I don't know if I can handle both Biology and Geometry. I feel better about Biology because I've always done pretty well in science.

Geometry is another thing. I think everyone fails Geometry. Algebra wasn't easy, but then I had Julie to help me. I do better when I have someone who will tutor me. Someone who knows the right answers. I don't cheat, but it's like having an answer book. You can check to see if you're learning things right. I don't see how I can pass Geometry, but it made my counselor happy to have me in "college prep" classes and I can always drop Geometry if I need to. I signed up to take it fifth period, I figure the later the better. Besides, there might be some cute guy in that class (David took Geometry) that I'd never meet unless I was in the same class. Maybe he would tutor me. I guess I'll just have to wait and see.

Chapter 2

ào

Keeping Your Options Open
(Larry's thoughts—September 14)

S hit man, who does this guy think he is? You can't run a class like that. How's he going to get away with this? Mr. Healy's a teacher. He can't just throw things out if he doesn't like them.

Today was the same old boring start of school. The only good thing about it is, it's the last year I'll ever have to worry about. Being a senior has all of the advantages, and none of the hassles. No one tells a senior what to do. We tell all of them what to do. I like it that way. Anyway, except for Band, which is always fun, today was a fairly normal, incredibly boring first day until I got to my fifth-period class.

Hey, I'll admit it, I'm not college material, but I have to keep my options open. I took Geometry fifth period with some of the other guys in Band, just in case I need it to get into college. It's not as if I'm expecting to go on, but like I said, you've got to keep your options open. I'm going to make a million dollars in real estate and you don't need college for that. Actually I don't care what I do, but it has to include making a lot of money.

I registered for Geometry just in case. I figured if I took it last period with the other guys from Band it wouldn't be so bad. Heck, it might even be fun. A lot of the people in Band are just what everyone says they are, "band geeks." They don't have a life outside of their precious instrument, but those of us taking Geometry aren't geeks.

Lunch was the same garbage they serve every year. I wonder if this was actually last year's leftovers or if there's some company that packages new garbage year after year. Anyway, after lunch I took a rest in my fourth-period shop class. By the time fifth period comes around, I'm ready for some fun. We're all sitting in fifth period, waiting for the teacher's patented first day speech about hard work, dedication, and effort.

The dude starts out, "I'm Mr. Healy, and this year in Geometry …" and I break in saying, "We aren't going to have books."

It was great. I couldn't wait to see what he'd do. It's the first day of class, he doesn't even know my name, so what's he going to do? I figure it's my responsibility to test out each teacher in the first few days. Everyone else expects it from me and I didn't want to let anyone down. Hey, it's a dirty job, but somebody's got to do it. I didn't know what to expect, but who cared? It was the end of the first day and if he couldn't handle it, so what?

Instead of getting on my case or sending me out of the room like a normal teacher, this guy says, "Okay, we won't have any books." Shit, what's wrong with this dude? Who's going to run this class—him or me? He's got to be tricking us; we're not going to have a class like Geometry without a book. This is serious stuff here. I couldn't care less what happens in the class, but there are other people who think that Geometry is going to be important to them. They aren't going to be able to function without a book. Is this guy on drugs or something? He's playing with the future of people here. The people in the class that are planning on going to college can't afford to have a teacher who messes around. I know they're hard up for math teachers right now, but this guy shouldn't be teaching.

Whatever happens, it doesn't matter to me. I've got it all figured out. I don't need college or anything. I've been planning it for years. The big money is in real estate and the lottery, but the odds against winning the lottery are about fifty million to one and it's all paid for by the losers. But anybody can make it in real estate, and I'm going to get my share of the big money. I figure I'll make my first million dollars within ten years after I leave this place. Then I'll buy a mansion on the ocean somewhere, have a bunch of servants, and retire to the good life. These other idiots going to Mountain View have no idea what they're missing. Unless they're the one in fifty million, after high school they'll go nowhere. Ten years from now that's exactly where they'll be—nowhere. That's not for me. As soon as I get out of this place I'm going for the bucks. Someone should tell these poor slobs what they're missing. Someone should open up their minds to what's out there and how to get it. Someone should do that, but it's not me. I'm going to look out for myself.

Not all of my friends are going to be rich like me, but I figure I can help them out after I make my money—if they really need it. Take Enoch, for example. He's a nice guy, but he'll never go anyplace with his ideas. He needs a mind like mine and the drive to go out and get what he wants. The poor wimp spends too much time thinking about other people and caring about what happens to them. I'm not putting him down for feeling that way, but it sure isn't the road to success. He's got to get his priorities straight. Before he goes around caring too much about other people, he needs to be a millionaire. Money first, then people later. He's a nice guy for a friend, he's just not going to be a success thinking the way he does.

The band is full of people like Enoch. Good, hard-working people, but shit, they won't get anywhere doing that. I don't mean to be selfish, but it's reality, man. If you don't look out for yourself, who's gonna do it? Take D and D [Dungeons and Dragons—a mind game played with dice and your imagination], you've got to see your situation and react to it if you're going to survive. I've been a Dungeon Master [the creator of situations and circumstances] for two years and I know you've got to keep thinking to stay alive very long in D and D.

You can't be a good DM if you try to do it alone. I keep in contact with other DMs by computer. You have to be informed what other DMs are doing if you are going to be really good at it. It's like real estate, you can't do it by yourself. D and D is good practice for my future. Everything was perfect until my computer contact with the other DMs broke down. But that's okay, you have to be ready to handle things yourself. No matter how well you plan for the future, you never know when you'll be on your own.

In D and D, the characters who don't look out for themselves don't last very long. You've got to be careful and you've got to be able to adjust to what happens during the game. The DM gets to create unexpected situations and see how the characters react. If they aren't ready, or if they aren't concentrating, they'll be terminated. You've got to save yourself. You can't depend on the others to do it. They're too involved living their own lives and saving themselves.

Anyway, back to this geometry teacher, he comes into class and lets me determine the future of all the students in the class with one little "welcome back to school" interruption. He's going to gamble their lives on the word of one student. There's got to be a law to stop him. I don't want to be responsible for the grades of all the students in that class. I can't help it if he's acting crazy.

They can't blame it all on me. They signed up for that class and they should have known better. You just can't trust guys like Healy. I may be responsible for the direction of the class, but I didn't make any of them sign up for that class, except maybe Enoch and Gerardo. And it's not my fault Healy decided to listen to me. How was I to know what he'd do when I said that? Shit, no teacher in the past has ever listened to me, so what's wrong with this guy? No matter what happens, I know it's not my fault, so no one should blame me.

It's not exactly true that no teacher in the past has listened to me. They listened to me until they kicked me out of their class. This time there was no kicking out of class, there was no argument, Healy just agreed... no books. I don't like it when someone who should be pissed off isn't.

I get pissed off when I should. My sophomore year at Mountain View I really lost my temper at the shop teacher. Hey, the dude had been capping on the band people in his class all year. The band people get along and understand each other and we like to take classes together. We have a different sense of humor and not everyone understands us, but we have fun just messing around. The thing about that guy was he didn't understand our sense of humor. He was always calling us "band geeks" and making fun of the group of us in front of the class. We may mess around a lot, but we put in the time. When it comes time for competitions we work our butts off. You don't bring back trophies from every competition like we do unless you're willing to put in the work.

Anyway, I put up with that guy capping on all of us, except for the time he got on Carlos, our freshman drum major. On the only Saturday competition the shop teacher happened to see, Carlos didn't do well. The Monday after the competition, that teacher really got on Carlos's case. Carlos didn't know what to do. The dude just kept on coming. He was destroying Carlos and wouldn't stop. Finally something inside of me just snapped and I went crazy. They say I hit him, and I hope I did, but I don't remember it at all. It's just like I blacked out or something. All I know is, people who don't know what they're talking about shouldn't criticize. I think people can treat each other better. Just because someone is a teacher doesn't give him the right to say anything he wants. He deserved it and I gave it to him.

I may not have been right, but I wasn't wrong. The principal suspended me for a week. My mom had to come in for a conference before they'd let me back in, but it was worth it. It really makes me mad when someone like Carlos is getting shit on and there's nothing they can do about it. They can't admit it, but I know the school agreed with me, because that teacher was gone the next year.

My mom backed me up like moms are supposed to do. I always know I can depend on my mom every time there's a hassle. Maybe she doesn't know what else to do, but she knows that it's her job to back me up. I guess I've given her enough hassles, but that's what being a parent is all about. I don't have any brothers or sisters— maybe that's why. Anyway, I think if you choose to have kids you're in for a lifetime of hassles. If you decide to have kids, you better enjoy hassles. I don't think I'll ever have kids. They're a pain. I don't know how I'd put up with someone like me. I'm going to live in that mansion on the beach with a dozen girls around me and no kids to hassle me. It sounds good and I can make it happen.

I think a person is pretty much in control of their own future. Take me, for instance. I know what I want and I know how to get it. I can see where I'm going and I can change anytime I want. But you've got to be smart and keep your options open. You always have to be ready to react to any situation. That's why I signed up for the geometry class in the first place.

I mean, what if I don't like selling real estate? I don't want to get stuck in a job where there's no fun. So I figure I can always be a lawyer if real estate isn't fun. I can out-argue anyone, and I'm not dumb. But if you want to be a lawyer, you've got to go to law school. To go to law school you've got to go to college. So I'm taking Geometry to cover myself. If I don't like real estate, I'll go to college, get into law school, and bingo, I'll be a lawyer. And no flunky lawyer either, I'll be a corporate lawyer and make the big bucks. A person's got to be prepared and keep their options open, if they're going to be successful in life.

Chapter 3

ze

Good Luck Warnings
(Chip's thoughts—September 18)

I t couldn't have been better if I'd planned it. The first day in my experimental No Book Geometry class was beyond anything I could have imagined. It was all due to the student that the teachers in the mathematics department had warned me about. ("Oh, you've got Larry in your class. Good luck.") Having been a teacher for fifteen years, I've had my share of "good luck" warnings, and the challenges they present are one of my favorite parts of teaching. Working with young people is my strength and my passion. I know teaching isn't for everyone, but there's no other job I would rather have. When the bell rings and the classroom door closes, I am my own boss. My evaluations arrive in the eyes of my students daily and in the report cards I write every quarter. I looked forward to meeting Larry with the same mixture of excitement and trepidation that I always had when I got a "good luck" warning. So I knew before he walked in that Larry had to be different from the others.

I try to be careful not to judge a student by the attitudes of his former teachers. I respect their opinions, but I don't believe that a student will be a problem for me simply because he was difficult in a previous class. There may be many reasons why a given student causes problems. Whatever the reason for the warnings about Larry, I'm sure glad he was there the first day of class.

Fifth period began normally enough. I was up front going through the patented first-day introduction to my fifth-period class.

"I'm Mr. Healy and this class is Geometry. This year in Geometry—"

At this point Larry interrupted, "—we won't have any books?"

Larry's interruption was just intended to get a reaction from me. I'm not sure what kind of response he expected, but I know that what he got wasn't anything like he had imagined.

I said, "It sounds like an interesting idea to me. Okay, let's do it. This year in Geometry, we won't have any books."

His interruption couldn't have been more timely. Now the other students don't know what to do with Larry and he doesn't quite know what to do with himself. Everyone thinks it was Larry's outburst that transformed that class into some kind of alternative form of geometry experience. None of them suspects I had already planned for it to be a bookless class.

After my introduction that Larry interrupted, I broke the class of twenty into five groups of four. I gave each group a piece of lined paper with a statement on it. Some groups got the statement: "Parallel lines never meet." Other groups got either "Triangles have 180 degrees," or "A linear pair has 180 degrees." I told them to pick a person to act as recorder and write down any thoughts that the group came up with after reading the statement on their paper. The interactions and discussions that took place in all the groups were extremely animated, and the papers they turned in indicated that they really were involved in what they had been given.

There were all sort of responses on the sheets they turned in. The comments ranged from "then non parallel lines do meet," to "each line must have 60 degrees," to "parallel lines are sexy."

In the first week this approach has created quite a bit of extra paperwork. While paperwork usually drives me crazy, I don't mind this kind so much. Especially if it is teaching them to think. Each night I go through the information that they turn in. The next day I give each group another sheet of paper. The topic or statement on the top of this sheet is one that I found on one of the sheets that was turned in the day before. It's been a lot more work than I expected because the class can't continue unless I read all the information each night and make up the investigation sheets to give back to the groups the next day. There are no easy preps, and this week they have given me far more information each day than I could use the next day.

The class time has gone by quickly because I'm always being asked questions or consulted about a possible discovery. I don't know where it will end, but this week was like a dream: excited, involved, questioning learners. It's not perfect. One frustration is the number of times they ask me what "real" geometry says about a topic they are discussing. I've avoided answering each query; I think if the experiment is going to be valid, I have to avoid adding any input. Even though my lack of input has been frustrating for some of them, it certainly has made them interested in learning geometry. It's so unusual for them because they are used to the teacher being the fountain of knowledge. They have an understandably difficult time adjusting to the source of the fountain being within themselves and each other.

Right now, it seems like it's going too well. The topics they investigate each day come from the papers that were turned in the previous day, but if they should decide not to turn in anything one day there would be no work for the next day. The class could self-destruct in a 24-hour period if they refused to investigate the topics they were given. There are so many things I can't predict or control about this class. Not only is it without a textbook for guidance, but there is no way of planning, except on a day-to-day basis. The responsibility is on their shoulders, and I have no recourse except to call off the entire experiment if I see it failing. It's difficult to give up control to the students after all these years of being the one in charge of the subject in my classroom.

I believe high school students can handle a great deal of responsibility if it is given to them. I sure hope I'm right, but, right or wrong, it's begun. I've given them the responsibility of an entire subject in high school. If we expect kids to act responsibly in life, they've got to be given responsibility from which to learn.

Responsibility is a tough subject. In some cases in the past I think I have used delegating responsibility as a cover for my laziness. I've wanted to avoid hassles, such as grading every homework assignment, so I've "shared" that responsibility with my students. That's not what young people need. They need the experience of accepting real responsibility in an environment that has certain safeguards, that will let them experience failure and success so that they can learn to handle both. They need someone there, not to rescue them should they fail, but to pat them on the back and give them encouragement to keep going and take on responsibility again. That's what I have to do in this class: let them experience responsibility, success, and failure. Perhaps more learning will come out of this class than just geometry.

It seems I've put myself in the same environment that I hope to create for the students. No one at the school except for my colleagues Ken and Yvette knows about the bookless class. Both of them support me 100 percent in this experiment, regardless of the outcome. The success of the class may be in question, but the support I've received from Yvette and Ken can't be questioned. Taking risks is easier if you've got a support system. Even if the idea fails, I know they'll be behind me. Some people are natural risk-takers and others are natural support people. I think we need to be a little of both if we are going to be truly happy and successful.

Anyway, the students seem to be really enjoying the freedom to discuss and research their own thoughts. Some are legitimately concerned that they won't learn enough "real" geometry to succeed in future math classes and the SAT test. It bothers me, too, but despite my concerns I'll never let them know I'm not sure of the experiment. I won't let them know about the books that I'm keeping in the cupboards in the back of the class in case the concept fails. I just keep giving them positive feedback for everything they "discover," and all week I've tried to reiterate my confidence in their abilities to succeed in an environment of discovery. They are doing better so far than I'd ever expected. Perhaps they are just responding to the new format, and the success won't last. Or perhaps, with the help of "good luck" Larry, they have stumbled on a special way to think and educate themselves. It's a risk I'm willing to take.

Chapter 4

ﻪ

The Possibilities
(Edmund's thoughts—September 20)

I t's not easy being the youngest person in a family like mine. My sister and two brothers get all the attention. They're the ones who accomplish things, and no one thinks that I can come up with anything that they don't already know. Education and knowledge have always been important in my family. My oldest brother is going to be a doctor. He's in his second year at the UCLA School of Medicine. My other brother had a 4.0 last year as a freshman at Stanford. As if that weren't bad enough, my sister is a senior at Mountain View and she's probably going to be valedictorian. I'm proud of them, and I know they are all involved in their own lives, but they don't seem to even recognize me as a real person.

Three years ago when we came to the United States from Korea, my father said everything was going to be great. And it has been great...for him. My oldest brother was already here attending UCLA when my father decided to move. I think my father wanted to be nearer to his son. I guess I can understand that, but it took the rest of us away from the lives we had in Korea.

My father could afford to move here because he's very smart. He is always successful in business, so it didn't matter what he did, we'd always have enough to eat. The last three years we haven't been as rich as we were in Korea, but now that he's got his own business there's plenty of money. In fact there's too much, because now he's thinking about moving to a richer city nearer to his business. I don't have many friends here like I did before we moved from Korea, but I still don't want to move again.

I really like reading and learning about things. It took me a long time to read English well, but as soon as I did, I began reading everything I could. Learning to read was very important to me, because there's so much information in books waiting to be learned. I've only been able to read "real" books for about a year.

I enjoy reading, but my favorite subject has been mathematics ever since I can remember. I think it's easier for me than it was for either of my brothers. I look forward to each new challenge in mathematics. That's why I couldn't wait to take Geometry this year. My sister told me that the hardest thing about Geometry was all the reading that was involved. This year was going to be a great year for me, because I knew I was ready for the reading and the challenge of Geometry. Algebra was easy for me, but I knew Geometry would be more of a test of my ability.

This year as a freshman in high school I've had trouble just finding my classes. This school is so much bigger and more spread out than my junior high was. The first day was very difficult for me because I don't have many friends to help me out. I'm kind of a loner. When I finally got to my geometry class fifth period, I was tired and just glad to get to the right classroom. The seats were in groups of four instead of rows, but other than that, it was a normal class. Except in junior high there were all these things on the wall to look at and learn about, but in the geometry class there wasn't anything on the walls—not even any theorems or axioms of geometry. But that wasn't the biggest difference from junior high. The first day, Larry, one of the students, interrupted Mr. Healy, the teacher, and told him we weren't going to use geometry books.

At the time I was shocked that Larry had interrupted, and even more shocked when the teacher agreed to not use a book. Now I think Mr. Healy just planned all along not to use books. How could a real teacher let a class be determined by a student, unless the teacher was already thinking about working without a book?

He's not the kind of teacher I expected as a geometry teacher. My algebra teacher was so strict and had all the facts that we were supposed to know printed up for us. She told us exactly what problems to do and which ones not to do. It worked out fine for everybody. I got an A in the class pretty easily. This geometry teacher is a different sort of person. He doesn't wear a suit or tie—actually he wears jeans a lot. He doesn't lecture to us, nor does he tell us what's right and wrong. Mostly he jokes around and gets to know the people in the class. It's so different than what I'd thought it would be.

The first day after Larry came up with the idea of having no books, Mr. Healy gave each of the groups different facts and told the groups to write down anything that we came up with. We could just use our brains to think about things any way we wanted to. I've never been able to do that in school. What we are doing seems very strange, but for me this is the most exciting thing I have ever done. I can think anything I want and there are no wrong answers.

Like on the first day, our group was given the fact that "parallel lines never meet." Larry was in my group and he said, "Parallel lines are sexy." I thought that was stupid and shouldn't be written down, but Mr. Healy's instructions were to write down anything, and

Larry is so demanding that I didn't disagree. The next day in class Mr. Healy even mentioned statements like "parallel lines are sexy." He said that any ideas need to be written down, because you never know how the idea may make others think. So I have no limits on me, I can think about anything—even something that has nothing to do with the thing we are given to talk about. I don't know if we should be given freedom like this in a class, but I know I like it.

It's been two weeks of this sort of thing with no guidance from Mr. Healy. It's perfect for me, but not everybody is into the idea of working this way. I know Mr. Healy thinks we can do it, but I don't think he's thought of all the consequences. What would he do if someone decided not to work, or if we failed to come up with the right information? I'm worried that we won't learn real geometry. If we don't learn real geometry, we won't do well on the SAT tests. And if that happens, we won't be able to get into a good college.

I think this class is the best thing that ever happened to me, because I can learn the information I'll need for the SAT test and college from books I read outside the class. I may never have another class where I have the freedom to think anytime I want to. Not only is there freedom to think, but the people in my group listen to everybody. They treat me as if what I say is important.

It's weird, the only ones in the class that know anything about real geometry are two students who failed Geometry last year. The first week of school everyone relied on them for information, but that's not so true anymore. We think they wouldn't have failed last year if they knew real geometry. Besides, the stuff we're coming up with is our own geometry. I like that.

Chapter 5

ેુ

Organization
(Alicia's thoughts—October 2)

O kay, I'm a perfectionist. I want to have everything in order. It makes life easier if you know where everything is. You know, some people just don't care. They do a mediocre job and feel satisfied that it's done.

Well, that may be good enough for them, but I want things to be done right. Why do something if you're not going to do it right? I think that's why I'm so good at the piano. When I have a new song to play, I do it over and over until I have it just right. I've been taking piano since the fourth grade and I probably drive my family crazy with all the time I spend practicing each piece, but they understand.

My parents taught me to always "aim for excellence." And they don't just give me advice or watch me, they support me in all the things I do. You know, I'm lucky to have them for my parents. Last year when I was student-body president of the junior high school, they were there for all the dances and all the activities where parents were invited. Even when it wasn't convenient, one of them would always be there. And that wasn't easy, because before I got elected, I promised the class if I were president we would have more activities than ever before at Baker School. And I live up to my promises. I figure if you're going to make promises, you need to keep them. Otherwise why make promises in the first place? The first dance of the school year was the first Friday of school and I really wanted it to be something special. So we had to meet in the summer to organize it. The school didn't let us hold meetings there, so we had all the meetings at my house.

I'm proud of my family and I'm proud of our house, but it's not a big place. For us to have meetings there wasn't easy. My mom kept my brother and my little sisters out of the meetings, and she even bought drinks and made cookies for everyone. We thought up some really crazy ideas that summer. My favorite was the Winnie-the-Pooh Dance where everyone comes dressed up like one of the characters. But we also came up with Future Teachers Day where different students got to teach the classes, a "gone fishing" ditch day, a lunchtime dunking booth where the teachers would be the ones dunked, and a bunch of other stuff. The house may not be big, but it didn't limit our imaginations. The principal limited some of our ideas, but nothing could stop us from imagining.

The only real problem with our house is it has just three bedrooms: one for my parents, one for my brother, and the three of us girls share the other one. Alex is lucky being the only boy in our family, because that means he gets a room to himself. You know, Alex is the best brother anyone could have; it's not his fault he's the only boy. But I'm kind of jealous of him, and I wish I had a room to myself. My little sisters are five and eight and they can't keep the room clean. It's not their fault. They're just little kids, but it really bothers me that my room can never be clean. Alex keeps his room just the way he likes. He's one year older than me, but we're both freshmen this year because I skipped third grade. It means I'm one of the youngest freshmen at my school, but it doesn't bother me because I know I can do it. In fact, being one of the youngest is a challenge to me and it helps me to work harder.

Being in the same grade as Alex has some advantages. When we were in junior high it meant we had some of the same classes, including Algebra. When we were at home we could study together. I think it helps both people when they are able to study together. Alex and I don't have a really big competition with each other, even when we're in the same class. We like to see each other do well. We kind of unofficially keep track of how we compare in school...at least I do.

Our Algebra teacher in junior high made us think that Geometry in high school was going to be really hard. But I really thought I was prepared for anything I might get in a geometry class.

Because I registered for Advanced English and tried out for Tennis, I couldn't take Geometry the same period as Alex. It turned out that the only geometry class he could register for was with a different teacher. Our counselor told us that it didn't make any difference because they used the same textbook for all the geometry classes. So we thought we were set up to be able to study math together just like last year, even though we weren't in the same class.

Surprise—my geometry teacher decided to change the whole approach to the subject. He said that if Euclid could build geometry thousands of years ago, our class in the eighties could do it too. It certainly isn't the same class my brother is taking. In fact Alex's class began in one book and just last week changed to another book. I don't have to worry about Mr. Healy switching books, because we don't have books to switch. We're doing geometry without a text.

You know, the whole idea of building geometry from the bottom up is a fascinating one. And it might be possible, if the students in the class were all A students. But the way it is, I really doubt it. There are all different kinds of students in that class. The only things we have in common are the class we registered for and a passing grade in Algebra. The people in the class are all different grades and they have such different personalities. It might have been an okay idea with an honors class, but I don't think we have very many modern-day Euclids in this class.

And Mr. Healy won't give us any hints if we are on the right track or if our thoughts are totally mixed up. It's really difficult to see how we are going to learn real geometry, but I do like the idea of a teacher having the confidence to let us experiment.

Mr. Healy is a nice guy and I guess he knows his geometry (but how will I ever know?), but he's not very organized. In fact, if it weren't for my notes, whatever it is that we've learned would have been lost. Our homework assignments are to find definitions for words that have come up in one of the groups during the day. Sometimes there's no homework, and other times there's a lot. When we turn the homework in, one of the groups reads all the assignments and develops a single group definition for each word. Then the next thing that happens is Mondays.

Sometimes I wish Mondays in Geometry didn't exist. On Mondays, the group definitions are put on the board for everyone to see along with our newest Discovered Truths [aka theorems]. "Discovered Truths" are statements which one of the groups discovered to be true about geometry. For example: opposite angles [aka vertical angles] are congruent. Then Mr. Healy reads each definition or Discovered Truth and the class has to agree on it, or change it until an agreement can be reached. It doesn't sound that difficult, but there are certain people who really care if a definition says what they think it should and others who are very adamant on some of the Discovered Truths. I don't think there is anyone in the class who hasn't spoken up at least a few times. It's hard to believe that getting the exact right wording is so important to everyone.

The worst part of the whole process is that the definition or Discovered Truth the class agrees on becomes a fact in our book, even if Mr. Healy knows it isn't correct. How are we supposed to learn the geometry Alex is learning if no one ever tells us if we are on the right track? I know Mr. Healy thinks this is a good idea, but how does he know it will really work? And why doesn't he give us some idea if we are right or wrong?

Whether we are right or wrong wouldn't make any difference if it weren't for me. Mr. Healy is so disorganized that he never writes down what our final decision is on the definitions and Discovered Truths we come up with on Mondays. In fact he's been relying on my notebook ever since he found out I keep notes on Mondays. Organization isn't one of his strong points. I'm not sure what his strong points are. He doesn't teach us anything, he only provides us with materials like the computer and the *Supposer* disk, rulers, paper, building materials, etc. He won't help us know what's right and he hasn't kept very good track of what has gone on in the first few weeks of school. He's lucky I was in his class, otherwise whatever things were decided on would never have been recorded.

The other thing he doesn't know much about is the computer. Sure, he knows how to turn it on and boot up a disk, but I don't know if he's ever even looked at *The Geometric Supposer* disk. One of the boys in the class, Gerardo, who is very comfortable with the computer, figured out the *Supposer* or we'd be totally lost. The *Supposer* is really important for two reasons: (1) The *Supposer* is part of real geometry and it answers questions with real answers. (2) It's got some real vocabulary words; too bad there aren't any definitions.

Not only does Mr. Healy not know The *Supposer*, he doesn't know how to use a word processor. He has the Appleworks® program, but he can't input the information. So not only do I keep a written record of all the class comes up with, I input it into the computer and save it on a disk. You know, I think he's irresponsible. He expects us to do everything.

How could a teacher get to this point? He's playing with my future. Geometry is an important subject. My father says it was the toughest course he took in high school. And he had a book! I like things to be organized and to be set up so anyone could follow them, but this class can't be done that way. I feel really uncomfortable every time I go into that class. Nothing is for sure except for the three things he gave us the first day, the "Given Truths." The entire class could self-destruct any day, if the students wanted it to. What would Mr. Healy do then? He'd have spent all this time playing with our future and we'd be the ones to lose.

I don't care what he says, I'm going to start looking at Alex's book when the tennis season is over. Then I'll know real geometry, and I won't have to worry about what's right and wrong.

I can't see how this class is ever going to be successful without anyone telling us what is right. Yesterday I did some checking. I went in to my counselor and just kind of talked about things in general. I can do that, because teachers and counselors have always liked me. They know I'm a good student and I think it makes them feel good to be around someone who is successful in school. Anyway, I finally managed to work the topic around to Mr. Healy without being too obvious. You know, I found out that he's been at Mountain View for four years. And he's taught geometry all four years, so he must know real geometry. I sure don't understand what he's trying to do. All I know is: without me in that class, he'd be lost.

Chapter 6

ૢ▲·

Just Throw Out the Texts
(Chip's thoughts—October 15)

I still hadn't told anyone about the No Book class except Yvette
and Ken, the kids in the class, and a reporter from the student
newspaper. After the article came out, of course, others knew.
That's how Bob, the principal, found out. I think I should have
warned him in advance.

Shawn learned of the No Book class from his friends in Band
and wanted to write an article for the school paper about it. I was flattered by the interest. Usually the school newspaper only came to me
for a quote for a track article, but this was different. When Shawn
came to interview me, I was ready for anything. I wasn't being excep-
tionally careful about choosing my words, thinking he could edit out
the parts he didn't want. He observed the class on two different days
and talked to Larry and Enoch about it.

When the article appeared, I didn't even get around to reading it. I did, however, read the article on child pornography, which
was printed directly above the No Book article. I wasn't the only person to read the child pornography article; it was of interest to all the

principals in the district. At the weekly principals' meeting they all commented on the article. The principal at our rival high school had also read the article beneath the child pornography piece. It began: "Mr. Healy didn't like the textbooks the district had given him, so he threw them out."

This other principal chided my principal, saying, "Do you let any of your teachers throw out the texts, or just this guy?" But Bob was unaware of the class, unaware of the article, and certainly unaware of the quote.

The day after the principals' meeting, Bob called me into his office to discuss the article, which I still hadn't read.

"So, Chip, how's the No Book class going?"

"Uh, fine."

"One of the principals was commenting on the article about your class in the school paper. Did you get a chance to read it?"

I didn't know exactly where this was leading, but I didn't think it was anywhere good. And I sure wished I had read the article.

Over the years, since the class I sponsored met the new principal with a shaving-creamed and toilet-papered campus, I have had frequent opportunities to apologize to Bob for things I've done. We've had our disagreements, but we agree that we both want what is best for the students of Mountain View. So our relationship has a rock-solid base, even if the disruption of the moment can be unsettling.

He had a copy of the school paper there for me to read (how convenient). He'd even highlighted in yellow the more significant parts. After he read the "throw out the text" part, I began the apology. When it got to the "why didn't you check with me?" part, I was well into my apology mode.

In the end Bob said he understood how the article came to be printed. He knew the student who had written it wasn't expecting other principals to read it. He even understood about the class, but was clear with his request to be kept updated on the progress of the students. Understandably, he was not pleased that I had failed to inform him about the class.

Communication. Even if I haven't done very well in that department lately, my students are learning it in the No Book class. They are learning to express their ideas clearly, so that everyone understands, and to really listen to each other. They aren't afraid to interact and ask questions.

Patty's presentation yesterday in class was an example of outstanding communication. She showed the class that a line could cross one parallel line without necessarily crossing the other. First, she went to the board and drew two parallel lines. Then she had a third line cross one line and stop before it got to the other one.

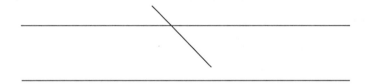

When the class said lines don't end, Patty was undaunted. She drew the same picture, except this time the third line crossed the first parallel line and then curved and stayed between the two parallel lines, never crossing the second.

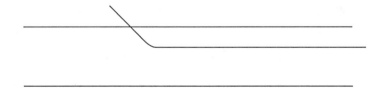

Then the class maintained that lines had to be straight and continuous. Patty thought for a moment and drew a third picture that began like the other two with a pair of parallel lines. The third line crossed one parallel, but avoided the other by "ducking" under it.

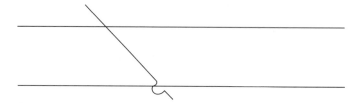

Patty had explained each picture and the class had understood each example. The discussion eventually led to the idea of a line segment, a straight line, and the concept of a plane. Patty had definitely learned to think and to communicate her ideas to others, and they had listened and responded.

Before Patty's demonstration the class had undergone some incredible turmoil with their definition of a line: "the path of a moving point" (like the exhaust from a moving car). The need for common definitions had arisen in the second week, and I decided on the spur of the moment to have the kids define terms as homework assignments. (This was actually a lucky break, as I hadn't determined yet what I could give for homework.) At the start of class, I stood at the door and collected their homework papers when they entered the next day. Everyone turned in a sheet, so I decided that definitions were good homework and have continued to give them out. After I collected the assignments, I graded them on a done/not done basis and assigned one group the task of reading all the papers and deriving a class definition for each term. Then each Monday I had the entire class review the previous week's class definitions. After several changes the class reached a consensus of opinion for each definition.

The class discussion leading to their final definition of line was remarkable. Seemingly everyone expressed his or her opinion. The whole class was determined to be involved in developing this definition. It was exciting to see how invested the students became in the accuracy of their definition, but at the same time I was concerned about the level of disagreement as they began to take sides in the argument. However, they did eventually reach a compromise that satisfied the different factions. The words straight and dimension could not be agreed upon and were left out of their final definition. One girl, who was repeating the class after failing a regular geometry class last year, agreed to the moving-point definition but said personally she couldn't see a line as not being straight. After all, she knew the book said a line had to be straight, and books are always right, aren't they?

When Ken found out that the class had decided a line didn't have to be straight, he also had trouble accepting it. He asked me if he could be a guest speaker in the class. He wanted to come in and set them straight (so to speak). Despite what I thought was a very logical argument from Ken, the students could not be budged. Their definition was going to stand. Even the girl who had originally disagreed wound up defending the class definition. It withstood every challenge, until Patty's picture.

But these everyday changes and the new definitions are really hard to keep up with. If Alicia weren't in that class, I'd be lost by now. She's keeping track of all the things we agree on. When I found out she knew how to use Appleworks (my word processor), I asked her to put the information on the computer. That was a big step toward organization. Now, each Monday after they agree on new definitions and "Discovered Truths" (that's their word for theorems), Alicia inputs them into the computer.

The "Discovered Truths" are ideas that groups have determined to be true and deem important enough that the entire class should be informed. When a group makes a discovery, they write it out and request that I put it on the board with the definitions to be voted on. The group that made the discovery usually wants to explain their reasoning, so the class introduction to a "Discovered Truth" has been basically a presentation of the fact and proof of validity. This is in contrast to the class discussion and class vote produced by each of Monday's definitions. Each time a definition or "Discovered Truth" is agreed upon, the class's bank of knowledge increases. If things keep going like this and Alicia keeps inputting them into the computer, by the end of the year we'll have made our own geometry book.

As if this class and all the new ways they have of looking at the world weren't enough, a week ago we got new textbooks for my other geometry class. Now I have my original set of definitions and theorems, the book we used last year, the book the fifth-period class is building, and the new geometry book. I don't have a clue as to the "real" definitions of anything anymore. Perhaps this is destiny. At least it keeps me from trying to direct the No Book class. They will develop their own "real" geometry just as the authors of other geometry books have been able to do. The only difference is that the things these kids develop will be their own. They've developed some pride in what they have discovered so far. They showed it when Ken tried to convince them a line has to be straight.

The first week they were so sure they weren't going to learn "real" geometry. They were sure they couldn't rediscover Euclid's geometry on their own. They're still unsure, but their confidence in themselves and their classmates is increasing rapidly. At the beginning they relied heavily on the two people in the class who failed Geometry last year. Most of the students in the class felt these repeaters had some of that valuable "real" geometry knowledge. They felt these two could somehow save the whole class with the knowledge they gained from their unsuccessful experience the previous year. Though this feeling didn't last for more than a couple of weeks, it was a big confidence builder for the two who had failed Geometry before. By the end of September, however, the class began to think they could handle things on their own.

It's been five weeks since the start of school and I'm just about to give my second test. For the first test I read over all the information Alicia had on the computer and based the questions on that information. One major problem was that the kids had no book to study, but starting with this test I'm going to get a printout of their information and make copies of it for them. The first test proved that although the students originally voted in favor of the definitions, in some cases they actually didn't agree with the final definition.

The day after the first test was most interesting. When we went over the test, these differences of opinion came out. As a result many of our definitions were changed. It looks as if the only place I will have any input into what goes on in the class may be by asking the right test questions—questions that will cause them to reevaluate some of their definitions and Discovered Truths. If I can't change their minds, at least I can make them look at things again.

The experimental class is approaching the point of no return. Soon I won't have the option to turn back and retreat into the books, because the kids won't have the time or inclination to learn the geometry presented in the covers of the book (new or old). I'm dealing with their futures. They are developing into thinking, interacting, confident characters, but are they on track to learn enough "real" geometry? The first progress report grades are due a week from Friday, and this class is going to present some interesting problems when it comes to grading. Their grades will be determined by two tests and the homework assignments (writing up definitions). Is that fair? There are so many unanswerable questions surrounding an experiment like this. People think that I have the answers to these questions and that my answers have some sort of authority. I just do the best I can. I don't know what the right answers are any more than the students in my class do.

This experimenting in the No Book geometry class has to be the most exciting thing I've done in the classroom since coming to Mountain View. It's so important that I do no teaching and give no input or opinions. If I gave them so much as an opinion at this point, they'd accept it as gospel, but I think they are getting away from that as time goes on. The first few weeks Larry would get so frustrated because he'd ask me a question and I'd refuse to answer it. He'd say accusingly, "You know the answer, don't you?" I never denied it, but it frustrated him. He had learned how to handle the educational system, but this class was outside all the rules in the system he'd learned to do battle with, and he didn't know what to do.

The number of questions they ask me is beginning to diminish. During the class I get to listen in on their conversations and ask an occasional question, but most of all I've become a go-fer. When they need to have materials like rulers, protractors, cardboard, colored pencils, sticks, construction paper, straws, paper clips, tape, or whatever, I locate them. That leaves the class alone in the room frequently. I open the door to the teacher next door (that covers me legally), but it's not necessary because the groups are so into their own projects and thoughts that they don't even notice I'm gone.

A few weeks ago I made a deal with Migrant Education. If they'd let me keep their Apple II® computer in my room, I'd let them use my room after school for tutoring. It was the only way I could get an Apple in my room. Now that I have the computer, we can use *The Geometric Supposer*, a program that will draw and measure just about any shape. When the kids learn how to use it, it will be an ideal system for experimenting. The *Supposer* wasn't intended for geometry the way they're approaching it, so sometimes it won't do what the kids want, but when it does it's great. I have to spend time helping them get used to it, and I end up watching as they investigate things.

This class is a whole different experience for me than anything else I've done as a teacher, but it seems to fit my personality and it's affecting my approach to my other classes as well. Last year I had a Basic Math class first period and it was a disaster. I used to count the number of people I had at the tardy bell each day. My record low was three, but the class never started with more than eight kids. So I asked Yvette for another first-period Basic Math class this year to see if I could find some way of getting them there on time. So far I spend most of the time in that class giving them positive feedback. Anything I can find to praise, I praise. I've told them they are my best basic class ever and I think it's true. (A self-fulfilling prophecy, perhaps?) Anyway, we're doing algebra in the class (I call it Algebra B—for Basic) and the kids are really enjoying it. It's not difficult algebra, just equations and some unknowns, and we still cover the regular material, but we begin every day with Algebra B. They like to see themselves being successful at what they view as a subject "beyond them."

Most people like to try to extend their skills. I think that's part of the reason for the success so far in the No Book class. They feel they are definitely in over their heads, but they are beginning to thrive in the land "beyond them."

Chapter 7

&.

Taking a Stand
(Chris's thoughts—November 3)

They just won't listen. How can parents ignore their daughter? What did I ever do to deserve the silent treatment I get at home? They only talk to me when they're mad at me. It's becoming more and more clear that I'm the burden in their life. It seems like they never get on the boys or Letty, just me.

The room Letty and I share is almost always neat and the boys' room is never clean, but the only person they criticize about their room being messy is me. When I get home from school, first I clean our room and then I clean the bathroom and the kitchen. I know I can't clean the whole house because everyone uses it. The boys always make a mess when they get home, so there's no reason to clean the living room. I wouldn't touch my parents' room anymore. The one time I did, my dad got really mad. He told me I had no right to go into their room and look through all their stuff while I was pretending to clean. I couldn't care less about their precious stuff. Besides, my father comes into my room any time he wants and he doesn't ask to go through my stuff, he just does it. I don't think it's right for a parent to do that. I don't think anyone has the right to go into someone else's room and go through their stuff. So I don't go into my parents' room or the boys' room. I think everyone should have a right to their own privacy in their room.

When I'm a parent, each of my kids will have a room of their own. They won't even have to share it with a brother or sister if they don't want. And when they shut the door, everyone will respect their privacy. Last night my parents and I got into an argument over me wanting to get a job (I don't think they'll ever let me work). My dad wouldn't listen to me. He just kept yelling and screaming about how ungrateful I am. When I told him he wasn't grateful that he had me for a daughter, he laughed in my face. I couldn't take it anymore. I ran into my room, slammed the door, and jumped on the bed crying. It didn't stop there. My dad practically ripped the door off the hinges when he came in and yelled at me for slamming the door in "his" house. Then he went through all my drawers and pulled out all my stuff and kept yelling about drugs and that he knew I hid them in my room somewhere. He said he knew I wanted to get a job just so I'd have money to buy more drugs.

Sometimes I can't believe him, he gets so crazy. But it's a lot better now than it was when he used to drink all the time. At least now he's always in a bad mood. When he used to drink he'd treat us real nice one time and give us presents, but the next time he'd hit us and threaten to do terrible things to us. He used to be an alcoholic, and we never knew what would happen. Well, according to the Alateen meetings he still is one, only now he's a "recovering" alcoholic. Things aren't perfect, but I have to keep reminding myself how much better things are now than they used to be.

Even though things are better, I don't understand why my mother stays with my dad. I've always wondered about that. She must think it's the right thing to do, or maybe she never considered any other making a decision.

Larry, this guy in my geometry class (no, I'm not attracted to him, he's just a guy), is always talking about keeping his alternatives open. That class is a place full of alternatives, so I guess it's a good place for a lot of people. I don't know how much geometry we're learning, but it's more fun than I expected. We kind of make up the class as we go along. When I say "we," I mean the students. There's no rules in the class, no right or wrong, no ultimates. I took the class to please my counselor and now it's my favorite. It's kind of the opposite of my house. In class what we say is important and we talk everything over before we decide on anything. I think people should talk things over—one person shouldn't be a dictator. Maybe the whole world couldn't function that way, but I think it would be a better place if people talked over their choices before they made their decisions.

And it's not just talking that makes a difference. Listening to what everyone has to say is just as important. The only person I expected to be listening to when I got into a geometry class was the teacher. I figured I'd just listen to the teacher, read the book and try to figure out how to do the problems, so I didn't look too dumb. In that class we don't have a book so there is nothing to read, the teacher doesn't lecture so we don't sit and listen to him, and we don't have to solve any problems (except on tests). We spend the time in groups investigating things and trying to discover things. Then on Mondays when we go over things, we decide what's important and what's not.

Last Monday we were going over our definition for the word distance. Almost everyone thought that it sounded good to say, "distance—the path between two points." But I knew that wasn't right, so I raised my hand. Mr. Healy hardly notices me. When I raised my hand I didn't even know if he'd call on me or ignore me.

Well, he didn't ignore me. When he called on me, I went up to the board and showed how distance could be between two or more points (like a triangle, or three points in a line).

It seems like Edmund and Larry always disagree, but this time both of them agreed with me. After a few people asked me questions, we voted on the final definition. What I had said must have changed their minds, because they voted to have "or more" in the definition. I know, the definition's not that big a deal. But it was a really big deal that people listened to me and actually cared what I said. They even thought that I was correct. When the whole class agreed on the definition, I felt great. In class, what I have to say is important, and people are willing to listen to me.

I think that's one of the things that made last night's hassle with my father so difficult. He won't listen to anything I say and he doesn't trust me. My dad won't even believe me when I say I'd never do drugs. He's always expecting I'll do all sorts of crummy things. I know who I am, and I know what I want to do.

Okay, sometimes even if I know what I want to do I make mistakes. Everyone makes mistakes. But I don't make mistakes when I feel really strongly about something.

I wonder if my father thinks I'm terrible because he used to do terrible things? Even if he did, it doesn't mean I'm going to be terrible or anything. I'm going to be me and he can't change that.

He thinks he has such control over me, but that's not true. I'm only going to be living at home for a couple more years and then I'm gone. I'll get a job and move out... or maybe I'll go to college. I might be able to do it, you know. If I set my mind to it I could. I know it.

Chapter 8

ઽ♣

The Plight of the PLIT
(Alicia's notes—November 14)

I think Mr. Healy is getting worse. Now he doesn't even have words for us to define. He draws pictures on the board of the thing to be defined, tells us to come up with the word and then define it.

Can't he do anything? I've been the one keeping track of everything that has gone on in class. I've been the one who inputs all the information into the computer to create this so-called "geometry book" we are making. I'm the one who keeps track of all the things that go on in class. It's hard enough as it is, but this last thing is going too far.

I've adjusted to not having a book and to developing our own definitions, and even to changing the definitions after someone finds an error. But creating our own words? Even if we do, by some miracle, learn real geometry from this crazy structure, and even if we learn some things about geometrical objects that the ordinary class doesn't, when we get to big tests, like the SAT, if we've made up our own words, we'll be lost. I know that; why doesn't he know it?

A few weeks ago Mr. Healy drew a triangle on the board and put an altitude in it.

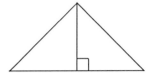

When he asked us to come up with a word for the line inside the triangle I figured he didn't mean "altitude," so I turned in the name "PLIT" (my acronym for Perpendicular Line Inside a Triangle). It was just kind of one of those things you do on the spur of the moment, not something I really expected anyone to take seriously. The whole assignment was ridiculous.

The group that looked at the homework assignments, and decided on the word and definition for the class to consider, liked the idea of PLIT. So next Monday (the day we consider things as a class to determine what will go into our "book"), the class discussed it. There wasn't the usual disagreement and they chose PLIT for their word.

Okay, I admit, I felt really good about it. Even if no one else knew where it came from, I did. And I had coined up something special for our book. It wasn't the word that everyone else knows, but it was my word.

Over the next couple of weeks some interesting things took place with my word. Naturally, Mr. Healy didn't say anything about us choosing a word that was different than the word the rest of the world uses. Because everyone knew what PLIT stood for, the whole class thought it was easier to remember—at first.

The next day someone in one of the groups discovered that a PLIT can be outside the triangle in obtuse triangles.

This wasn't a problem, we just added the term "PLOT" (Perpendicular Line Outside a Triangle) to our vocabulary the next Monday, and everyone was happy. This all took place about four weeks ago, and nothing else happened until last week. One group found out that parallelograms have a perpendicular line like the one inside of triangles. Larry said it was okay and coined up the word PLIP and two days later we added PLOP.

You know, I thought I had my values pretty well figured out as far as grades and school are concerned until Sergio brought up a question about our vocabulary words.

Sergio is a junior and he had an incredible football season. He's a babe—strong, good-looking, friendly, and probably not the least interested in freshmen girls. I don't know about the other girls, but there's no doubt in my mind which guy is the ultimate in that class. Sergio's not a particularly good student, in fact I don't know how he even got into a geometry class, but he does have the ability to kind of sift through all the garbage and find ways to simplify things. I'm not sure if it's because he's just lazy, or if he's really smart underneath. I guess he'd just had it with all the plits, plots, plips, and finally plops.

The next Monday, when we were trying to add PLIP and PLOP, Sergio raises his hand and asks Mr. Healy, "Why don't we forget all this PLIT and PLOP junk and just call an altitude an altitude?"

At first I was really hurt, because the support he got from the rest of the class meant that my word (and all the generations that followed) would be gone forever. It never meant all that much to me anyway. At least I didn't think it did, until I heard myself arguing in favor of keeping all the PL words.

I never thought I'd be arguing against anything that Sergio said, but it was kind of like a personal attack. Well, that's how I took it. So, I was arguing against the one person in the class I didn't want to disagree with. And I was arguing in favor of not having "altitude" in our book, which is exactly what I thought should have been done in the first place. If you told me two months ago that I'd be arguing against Sergio or against real geometry, I'd have said you were out of your mind. But you know, it didn't seem so crazy when I was explaining why PLIT was a better term for the concept of altitude.

At one point I said, "We are our own authors of geometry, and we don't have to be tied down by whatever the rest of the world believes to be true because this is our class." I don't think I really believe that stuff (maybe I do and don't even know it), but I sure was arguing like I believed it.

Now don't get the wrong idea. Right is right, and I do what's right. This class isn't going to change me. If anything's going to change, it'll be the class, not me. I'm going to learn real geometry because it's the knowledge that's important, not thinking, talking, or discovering so-called "truths" that keep changing. What we need is geometric knowledge and I'm going to end up with it, whether Mr. Healy helps or not. If you have enough knowledge you can do anything. If you have knowledge, people will respect you and they'll know you are a good person.

It's strange that I was ever affected by Sergio in the first place. He may be good-looking, but he isn't so smart, and he doesn't treat me or anyone so special. In fact, there are a lot of other boys better than him. Besides, I've never been affected by boys, they're just too much hassle. In junior high so many girls lived as if they were nothing without a boyfriend, and that's just plain stupid. You can be anything if you try hard enough and you're willing to learn what it takes. No boy or anyone can make you become something you don't want to be. You know, I think I'm a little anti-boys because of all I've seen in the last few years. It's not that I don't like them, or think about them. It's just that I'm not going ga-ga over them. And I'm not going to be controlled by what they think of me or by what they want me to act like. If they don't like the way I am, that's their tough luck.

But if I really feel that way I wouldn't have been thinking about disagreeing with Sergio, would I? Okay, I guess I am affected by some members of the opposite sex more than others and I'm definitely affected differently by boys than girls my own age. Moises and Gerardo (two of my boy friends) say I'm pretty, and I think they're being honest with me. But really, how do you ever know whether you are really pretty, or if someone is just saying that? You know, I don't think a person can ever really evaluate their own looks. Besides, whether I'm pretty or not doesn't even matter.

What really matters is whether or not Sergio thinks so. Wow, I sound like all those other girls who get so guy crazy. Well, I'm not going to be boy crazy. Sure I'd like Sergio and some others to notice me, but I won't let my life revolve around them and their opinions.

I used to think that I had all the answers and that my family had the right way to look at things. But when you live in junior high and now high school, no matter how well connected you are, no matter how straight you think you have your priorities, you get affected by the people you have around you. I've never felt that I was better than the other girls, but somehow I thought I would rise above the petty things that so many girls are run by. Maybe it's not that easy. Everyone is affected by people around them. Keeping your priorities straight isn't easy.

I think I could probably handle having a boyfriend like Sergio, but it's not the end of everything if he doesn't care. I'm happy to have friends and be involved in activities like tennis. The season is nearly over and I never made a varsity match, only JV. That's okay, because I only joined tennis to enjoy myself and the other girls on the team. I made a pact with myself not to get over involved in my freshman year like I did last year, but I don't think being on the tennis team is too much stress.

This year I'm just being me, and even if the PLIT and family didn't gain any fame, I know I can really make some contributions to that class. And not just the kind that come from keeping that poor Mr. Healy from losing everything we hand in to him. You know, I may not have made the best contributions to the discoveries in that class so far (I've done all the work and still only got a B+), but my biggest contributions are yet to come and they aren't going to be just as an organizer of an unorganized teacher. Just you wait and see.

Chapter 9

ટ▲·

Opening Minds
(Larry's thoughts—December 5)

I t's not my job to transport all these imbeciles to enlightenment. All right, I have an easier time than all the other people in the fifth-period No Book geometry class. They still think they can't come up with real geometry. I don't give a shit if we ever come up with real geometry, we're going to create a never-to-be-duplicated geometry. The trouble is, while I'm out there on the edge of universal discovery, the rest of them are lost somewhere in the most basic ideas ever to cross a classroom. This Healy guy didn't know what he was getting into when he gave me a chance to challenge anything that anyone ever came up with. Just watch me work.

The only down side of this whole process is we don't get to create alone, we're in groups. That means those of us who are more enlightened have to drag these other dolts kicking and screaming through the sea of creativity. I love it, but it seems like I have to be the raft on which most of my group depends for survival. It's not that I don't understand the position, but I'm not sure how to handle it all. I've been creating things ever since I can remember. It's one of the reasons I like being a DM in D and D. I enjoy stretching realities and questioning what is an actual law of nature and what was merely the whim of some idiot in history, who didn't know which way was up. Some of those guys established laws for unknown reasons, and the rest of us in history have had to memorize it and accept it as gospel.

Take the idea of a circle having 360 degrees. What good does 360 do, anyway? Why did they choose that number instead of 300 or 400 or some other number? What's so sacred about 360? I started thinking about it a long time ago, but I never said anything. I know how to get through school. Teachers don't want you to think about the world, they want you to memorize what they think is important about the world. If you can swallow the facts they want you to know and regurgitate it on one of their tests, you pass. If not, you fail.

Shit, I've known how to play the game since I was in elementary school. It's not one of the things I revere about education, but if you're going to play the game you've got to know how to win. Education is just a game—some people win and some people lose. You have to agree to play the game according to their rules because without an education you aren't worth shit in this world. I'm not saying I agree, but I know the facts. Until I'm in charge, I've learned to operate in their world. When I run the world, it'll function according to my rules.

We're making our own world in that geometry class. I never thought that class would be worth anything unless I wanted to go to college. I'm thinking about college more now then I ever did before, but the class is worth more than that. This class not only lets us challenge old facts, but it even encourages it. I'm not sure Healy would agree with all the changes we're working on, but he said it was our class and so far he hasn't interfered. I bet it's killing him.

Getting back to the 360-degree circle. When I told the group how ridiculous 360 degrees was, they just sat there and couldn't see what difference it made. So I told my mom, who works at the *Herald Examiner* newspaper, to find out where they got the idea of 360 degrees. Using her computer check system, she found a book in the fifth library she consulted. I went and checked out the book.

According to this book, sometime in the 12th century there were a bunch of scientists and mathematicians gathered together in Germany. One evening the mathematicians noticed the horizon appeared to be a circle from where they were standing. Meanwhile, an astronomer mentioned there were 360 stars visible. So somehow the idea got into the mathematicians that was how many degrees there were in a circle. Is that wild or what?

I don't know if it's true or not, but it didn't matter. When I took that information to my group and told them about it, you should have seen them. They couldn't believe the number of degrees in a circle was determined in such a useless way. Like I said, I don't know if I believe it, but that doesn't matter. With that information their closed minds opened a crack momentarily, and I took advantage of it. As soon as they noticed the possibility of some ancient law being fallible, I introduced the Metric Circle, which is based on 100 degrees. I helped them discover the wonder of my Metric Circle and the ease with which it could be used. They were ripe for indoctrination.

Here were these waiting minds ready to be filled, but it took so long to get to that point that I was nearly out of time. All year we have only been allowed to work with the same group for exactly two weeks. It took nearly that long for me to get my group to see the light. Healy was really stubborn about not allowing me to keep my group of semi-enlightened followers together for another two weeks. I finally convinced him to let me tell the rest of the class why our group should stay together for another two weeks. The final decision would be left up to the class members.

Last Friday was the day I told the rest of the class that my group needed to stay together. I'm not saying the rest of my group were wimps, but they weren't exactly dynamic, so I did the speaking for them. I presented the idea without telling the class exactly what we were doing. I didn't want the idea of the decade snatched out from under us. Maybe I wasn't Mr. Diplomacy, but the class attacked me from the very beginning. They wanted to know exactly why I wanted two more weeks and I tried to explain without giving anything away. They really frustrated me. They kept saying it was their class and if I was going to try to disrupt the format, they needed to know why. Well, it came down to a personality clash. They couldn't deal with what I was saying. Finally I let them know that it took me nearly two weeks to open up the minds of the people in my group and I didn't want to start all over again with a bunch of new closed-minded people. I told them I didn't even know if they were smart enough for me to open their minds. That pissed off practically everyone.

It was the truth, but wasn't real influential in our favor. The only one who didn't outright attack what I said was Chris. She said she didn't know if her mind could be opened, but she wanted the chance to see. She wanted the chance to be in my group so she thought we should change groups. I could probably open up her mind fairly quickly because at least she was receptive.

The vote wasn't going our way. Then Sergio said if what we were doing was so great, he wanted to hear from someone else in the group. That's when Carmen walked up to the front. I had no idea what she would say, but I was tired of the abuse I was taking. Carmen hardly said anything in our group, but at least she wasn't negative about our Metric Circle. She's tall, quiet, and not bad looking.

I don't know what it was about her, but when she talked in her soft voice, the rest of the class listened. It was the first time I'd heard her say two words. I don't remember exactly what she said, but I didn't care. All I knew is it calmed down all those people who wanted to lynch me. More than that, they were listening. It probably had to do with the fact that she was living proof that I didn't harm anyone. That my ideas were good, even if I screwed up the presentation. Carmen told them not to judge the idea on what I had said, but on the chance that what we were investigating was something really worthwhile. Shit, without me there wouldn't be anything to investigate. On the other hand, without Carmen's soft voice and convincing presentation, there wouldn't be a group. She convinced the rest of the class to give us one week. Then we'd present what we had, and the class could decide what to do next.

Okay, so public speaking isn't my strength; it can be developed. And it's not bad, if the audience isn't hostile from the start. If they learn how to listen, I'll learn how to make a good presentation.

Anyhow, tomorrow we begin our third week together because the quietest person in our group had the guts to stand up and convince the class. I think there may be more to Carmen than I thought. We're going to look into metric protractors, metric curve measurements, and all the consequences of the change. The rest of them don't have the vision for it, but I can see this becoming a national movement. Some people just think too small. If you've got a great idea that would benefit all of mankind, you've got to think big.

Chapter 10

ε⏳

Not for Everyone
(Carmen's thoughts—December 6)

Okay, I know I'm not the smartest girl at Mountain View. I've known I'm not smart since third grade, when we did math. I couldn't remember the times tables. I used to sit in the dining room for hours with those flash cards and my big sister, Josie. For some reason they just wouldn't memorize. And my teacher took advantage of that. It seemed like he was just waiting to find something to criticize.

I was used to criticism because Josie seemed to like to criticize almost everything I did. But she was my sister—I could handle it from her because I knew she actually liked me. We got along in most areas, especially when my parents were involved. I think she was too critical for them, too. She didn't get along very well with them, until I learned how to act kind of like a go-between. It helped my parents and Josie.

I've always tried to help people. Not because I was trying to be wonderful, but because it's made me feel good to see others happy. I guess that's the reason I've always had so many friends. I think having friends and being happy makes school a good place for you. I know it was good for me from the start of kindergarten.

I got along with nearly everyone and didn't have a problem with anyone until I reached third grade, where it seemed like Mr. Dell, the teacher, was out to get me. I couldn't make him happy, no matter how hard I tried. He was usually on my case about something, but the thing I remember most was the times tables. He'd always call on me to recite the eights, which he knew were my worst. I tried to pretend that it didn't bother me, but it really did.

When he handed back multiplication tests, he'd save mine for last and let everyone know what I'd missed. Maybe he thought it would make me learn, but it only made me hate math. That was when I started to write stuff. At least Mr. Dell gave me support in my writing. I think he had it in his mind that I couldn't do math because I was a girl. None of the girls did very well in math in his class. He only thought I could do things like writing. I think I was pretty good at it for a third grader.

Third grade was a real turning point for me; I learned to be afraid of math. Even though I did fairly well in fourth, fifth, and sixth grades in math, in junior high my math grades went down, but never below a C. I knew I couldn't do math after third grade. Every time we started a new section in math, I was always afraid. I kept waiting for another Mr. Dell and another eights times tables to appear. I guess it didn't, because I never found another thing where I had a block against learning it like I did with eights. I nearly thought I had reached that point in Algebra the last two years, but somehow I got through it.

My dream is going into big business after high school, and I don't see why I need more math for that. I wish that I could become part of a big corporation and see how things actually work. I doubt that I'll be able to do it, but it's what I always wanted to do. At least I figured I didn't need more math classes.

After Algebra, I wasn't planning on any other math classes for the rest of my life. I'd completed my math requirement for graduation and that was plenty for me. Then my counselor told me that because of the way I took Algebra (a one-year course spread over two years), I still had to take another math class for graduation. Even though graduation is still two years away, I wanted to get rid of that requirement. My choices were Consumer Math, for those who never did well in math, or Geometry, for those of us who passed Algebra. My counselor said Geometry was more reading and creativity, and wasn't so much math as the other class. I didn't understand how that could be, but I agreed to take the class and give it a try. I figured if I fail Geometry, I can always take Consumer Math next year.

Two of my things I'm best at are reading and creativity. I think my counselor knew that when she suggested Geometry, but I didn't care. I just liked to hear her suggest a course as hard as Geometry. Josie nearly failed it when she took it, and she got good grades in almost every class. She always complained about the reading assignments, so I knew that there was a lot of reading involved.

They say if you write stories you are probably creative (well, that's what good old Mr. Dell said), and for the past few years I've been writing stories in special notebooks I keep just for my stories. One is over ten chapters long and I'm not nearly finished yet. I created the story out of my own mind and I think it's really good. It's about a girl my age who runs away from the orphanage where she lives and goes to a big city and starts a new life. She really believes in herself and has the courage to face up to problems and she nearly makes it, except for this one thing that comes back to haunt her from her life before she ran away. It's fun to write and I hope maybe it's good enough to be published someday. That would be the neatest thing that could happen to me.

The best thing I thought could happen to me this year was in volleyball. If we could win more games than last year and not finish in last place again, I'd be happy. I was really ready to concentrate on volleyball. In fact, that's why I signed up for Geometry fifth period, because it's just before volleyball practice. So if I couldn't do the reading, I'd be able to take it out on the volleyball if I wanted to. I'm the tallest girl on the team, so I'm the primary spiker. I figured if Geometry were too hard, I could get my frustrations out on the court.

Well, the geometry course I signed up for doesn't have too much reading, that's for sure—there's no book! Of all the classes I could get into, I got to be one of the Mountain View guinea pigs, in this sort of space-age approach to geometry dreamed up by the teacher Mr. Healy. He's a far cry from Mr. Dell, but they both look kind of alike (maybe it's his nose). The difference is that Mr. Dell never had a kind word to say about anyone unless it really suited him, but Mr. Healy is always encouraging us to explore, and no matter what anyone comes up with he never says it isn't possible.

I never cared what he said because I didn't get really involved in the class. I'm barely passing (if that) and nothing would have changed except for the group of people I'm working with in the class right now. This one guy, Larry, thinks he's God's gift to geometry and it's his destiny to "open up the minds of those hopeless creatures in the class endowed with less intelligence." He reminds me a little of Josie when she gets into her "I'm number one" state of mind.

I tried to act as the translator for Larry's ideas to the other two people in our group, just like I do for Josie and my parents. I had to admit he had some good ideas, but the way he presented them wasn't very clear and it offended the two others in our group. He wanted to create a circle with 100 degrees, instead of the normal 360 degrees. Personally, I don't care how many degrees a circle has in it (I'm not even sure I understand exactly what a degree is.) But for our group to function, a translator had to be found who could explain the Larryisms to the group before he bit someone's head off. (I wonder if Mr. Dell was like Larry in school?) Larry got so frustrated when he had an idea that the others would refuse to consider or couldn't comprehend, but I knew how they felt. They were confused, like eights times tables. Sometimes your brain just won't accept things unless they are rearranged. That's what I did, I "rearranged" what Larry said.

We went through a week of Larry speaking to our group with me as the rearranger when it was necessary. I think the biggest problem was that the rest of the group could only think in one way (some people are more bound to tradition—like a circle has 360 degrees—than others) and Larry couldn't accept that. So it was anarchy or interpretation, and seeing as I get along with everyone in that group I was the natural link between them. By the end of the week Larry was convinced that we could discover and develop major improvements. Everyone in the group was involved in the whole idea and offering their suggestions. This must be the way decisions are made in big business.

Then, on the second Thursday of our time together, we realized our group needed more time to work with each other. Mr. Healy has this concept of discovery or something that says that we have to switch groups every two weeks. Sometimes it's good and sometimes it isn't. Larry and I went to talk to Mr. Healy about the idea of a two-weeks extension for our group, but he wouldn't change. But then he said he'd give us the chance to convince the rest of the class that our group should stay together for another two weeks. The class could vote on it and he'd agree with their decision.

So Friday, Larry made the presentation to the rest of the class. For some reason he refused to give the class information about our investigations—like he had some mysterious discovery. It was as if he had a corporate secret that would mean financial gain and he was afraid one of the others in the class might try to steal the secret from him if they found out too much. So Larry tried to convince them to let us stay together for two more weeks without giving them much information what we were up to. The class got kind of ugly and started to laugh at the idea, and Larry reacted in his "Larry" way of putting everyone else down. Somehow he thinks if he puts everyone else down, they'll agree with him. Either it doesn't work very well, or he doesn't do it very well. After Larry got through saying that he had "opened our minds and didn't know if anyone else in the room was intelligent enough for him to be able to open their minds" he lost virtually all the support he had started out with. I figured it was up to me to translate for Larry, the same way I did in our group.

I'm not the type who gets up in front of a group of people easily. In fact I hate it. But I had been making a real contribution to our group. I knew there was no way we were going to stay together if Larry was the last person the class heard before voting.

Larry walked back to his seat saying, "See if I care how you vote!" leaving the podium empty.

So I got up to "translate" again, only this time it would be in front of the whole class. I was so scared that when I started to talk you could barely hear me. Then the strangest thing happened. I saw the whole class was listening to what I said. I told them that we were working well together and that we had made some discoveries that we wanted to share with them, but weren't ready to yet.

I said, "We aren't keeping secrets, we just need time to verify our discoveries. If you vote to give us another week together, we will continue to work on the circle idea. And a week from today we will be ready to present the entire plan to you. Then you can decide if we will be given the second week together."

It sounded so good I couldn't believe it was me talking. Everyone listened. Better than that, they completely reversed their opinion and voted unanimously to let us have the week's extension. What a feeling!

After I finished and sat back down, do you know what Larry said to me? "In the two weeks we've spent together, this is the first time I've heard you talk."

Where had he been all the time I was translating for him? I guess listening isn't something he ever does. He's more into using people to accomplish things. Funny though, I don't feel used. It just feels good to know that I can help people learn.

I may not learn about geometry in this class, but I learned about me. I still can't do math, but I do have the ability to actually influence the way people think.

Chapter 11

≥▲,

*The Word Spreads
(Chip's thoughts—December 11)*

Things are changing. Ever since the No Book class started there have been more and more people interested in what happens in the fifth-period geometry class that lives in my room for an hour each day.

The people at PLUS (Professional Links with Urban Students—a nonprofit organization in the Los Angeles area designed to help math teachers understand the expectations of industry and college) and the involved schools have been fascinated by the entire concept. It's amazing the support I have felt in this undertaking. It didn't feel like I was doing such a marvelous thing when I began the No Book class.

One Saturday each month I attend a workshop on *The Geometric Supposer,* along with several other geometry teachers from high schools around the L.A. area. The instructor of the workshop heard about the No Book class through Toby (the coordinator at PLUS), and asked me to take class time at the second workshop to explain what I was doing. I couldn't believe the interest. I spent over an hour talking about it and answering questions. I still don't see this as something spectacular, but it clearly has some special value in the eyes of the geometry teachers in the area. I didn't like standing up in front of a bunch of adults to explain the idea. (Kids? Yes. Adults? No.)

It's never bothered me that I hold only a minor in math, but when I had to talk in front of a group of math majors I was intimidated. What if they asked me about mathematical things I'd never heard of? It was hard at first, but after I got into it, I forgot about that. In fact, I really enjoyed it because they became so involved.

A few weeks ago, Toby suggested that the reason I am able to run a class this way is because I'm not as particular as the usual math teacher. Perhaps that's why I could only minor in math. I never thought that might turn out to be a strength for me.

The workshops aren't the only place where other people are finding out about this class. Our school is a test pilot school for *The Geometric Supposer* and the new Sunburst book that goes with it. All the pilot schools are computer linked with a group called EDC (Education Development Center) in Massachusetts, which was hired to get feedback on the *Supposer* and the book. Through my computer and the phone lines, I communicate with the project leader, Grace. At MSTI I never expected to use the computer for telecommunications, but with the help of my MSTI roommate, Ken, I have begun to communicate in Computerese. Originally when Grace contacted me on the phone in the conventional manner, I mentioned my No Book class. Like so many others, she was fascinated with the concept. Now we communicate "on line" (that's Computerese for talking on the phone via computer) three or four times a week, and she has monitored the progress of the No Book class. I guess there must be a number of people living somewhere near Boston who are enthusiastic about this class.

One thing's for sure: the students in the class are enthusiastic. And they seem to be enjoying themselves. No matter which group I visit, their enthusiasm and involvement make it hard not to become involved in what they are talking about. I used to be the source of information and the kids treated me as if I held all the answers (little did they know I'm an explorer as much as they are), but now they treat me more as a facilitator (I think I like that term better than go-fer) for the class to function. They want to discover things for themselves. If they need materials for their investigations they come to me, but lately they've stopped bringing me their questions about geometry. Since they brought me down from the pedestal of knowledge on which they assumed I sat when they entered the classroom in September, they haven't decided if my input is worthy of note at present. Is this progress?

One of the major changes in the class happened last week when Larry tried to convince the rest of the class to give his group a two-week extension. He felt that a great deal would be lost if his group was split up at that point. Usually when Larry talks the rest of the class listens, even if what he has to say is worthless (in my opinion). His grip on the class was strong before he presented his case for the group staying together.

Larry tried to keep secret what his group had discovered. Because he was so secretive, the class began to reject his proposal. That upset him and he didn't know how to react. In frustration he responded with an air of superiority, which did nothing for his case.

Unfortunately for Larry, his presentation centered on his ability to "open up the minds of the people" in his group, which alienated the class. Almost in desperation he said, "We need to keep this group together because I'm not sure I can open up the minds of others in this class; they may be too stupid."

Calling the voters stupid is not likely to influence them positively. One girl said she wanted to have her mind opened and she felt it was unfair for Larry not give her a chance to be a part of his group. As a result, she was against the group staying together. The rest of the class just didn't want this person who called them stupid to have his way. I didn't intervene, but I sure felt like it. Especially after Larry stormed off the podium.

The podium was vacant until one of the other members in Larry's group, a girl who hadn't said anything all year, approached the front. She presented the same case, but from a different perspective. She suggested that the group be allowed to remain together for just one week, at which point it would produce results for the class to consider. Then, if it was necessary, a vote for a second week could be taken. Carmen had taken a nearly disastrous moment and reversed the public opinion so quickly no one knew what had happened. By the end of her couple of minutes at the podium, the vote was unanimously in favor of allowing the group to continue.

Interactions like these happen all the time in the lives of teenagers when there isn't a teacher or parent around to add discipline and order. Somehow they seem to get through them. This should serve as a reminder to me the rest of the year that interference by an adult is not nearly as necessary as we tend to think. And in a safe environment like the one that has been created in that fifth-period Geometry class, some beautiful things can happen. Everyone in that class is significant. No one can predict from which part of the room the next valuable piece of input may come.

One of the things I've got to do over Christmas break is sit down and really memorize which people in that class are which. The idea of switching seats every two weeks may be beneficial to the class's progress, but it hasn't been so good for me personally. I know people like Larry, Alicia, and Edmund a whole lot better than some of the ones who don't tend to offer as much. In fact, if I hadn't had Carmen in Algebra two years ago, I might not have even known her name. That's a big problem for me in that class. Oh well—it'll give me something to do between Christmas and New Year's.

Chapter 12

ε**▲**·

The Christmas Surprise
(Chris's thoughts—December 16)

My father took us to the fair last Friday night and it was fun, but it could have been a lot more fun if we'd been on our own. Letty and I met these two really cute guys, one was twenty and the other was sixteen. They were a little old for us, but we weren't planning on marrying them or anything. They worked at the fair operating the Ferris wheel for the entire weekend. And so Letty and I spent most of our time right there at the Ferris wheel, talking to them. Well, we couldn't even have a good conversation, because we were always worrying that my dad would come up and spoil everything. He was with the boys going on the other rides and playing the games. Julius can really throw a baseball well and always wins prizes at those "knock the bottles down" booths. My dad likes to watch Julius win things. I wonder if my dad was ever athletic like Julius when he was younger.

After Julius had won a big stuffed lion and two medium dogs, they came and found us at the Ferris wheel, where we pretended to be in line.

After we left that night, Letty and I were determined to go back to the Ferris wheel the next day, but not to wait in line. We wanted to go see those guys without my father there to spy on us. So we had to make up this elaborate story about how we got to know two little boys at the fair, how they really wanted to go on the Ferris wheel, but they were afraid. We said we had told them that we could take them tomorrow if they worked up the courage. We said we'd promised to meet them there at five o'clock the next day. I don't know if my dad believed the story or not, but he agreed to let us go back to the fair. He sure wouldn't have said okay if we'd told him the boys we were meeting weren't little boys. If we'd said they weren't afraid of the Ferris wheel, that they operated the Ferris wheel.

Mom took us over there at five and we got to just sit and talk with those two guys and they took us out for dinner on their break. Okay, for a couple of hot dogs, but it was dinner and they paid for it. That's all that happened. I was hoping for a little more, but I guess they weren't really interested. I was glad they didn't try anything, but I felt a little rejected too. Maybe it was because they were in charge of the ride and were responsible for it. Anyhow, they were a lot of fun to talk to without having to keep looking out for my father like we had the day before.

We got to the parking lot at 10 o'clock like we'd agreed to and waited for my dad. When he got there to pick us up, he was in a rotten mood. As soon as we got in the car, he began to get on our case. He said we didn't deserve to get to come back to the fair and that we were spoiled. That we thought we could do just as we pleased and didn't care about anyone else. Then he landed the big one on us. He told us that he had decided not to buy any Christmas presents this year for anyone in the family because no one deserved any.

I told him that wasn't fair. He just couldn't decide not to buy anything. (Am I spoiled?) My little brother still believes in Santa Claus. If there weren't any presents, it would really hurt him. My father said if I thought that was so important, I could play Santa Claus for him— which I'm going to do, no matter what.

Then I reminded my dad that he had promised Julius that he would buy him a Nintendo game for Christmas. That was the wrong thing to say because my dad said that he was still going to get the Nintendo game for Julius. Because Julius deserved it, and he wouldn't deprive him of a gift if he deserved it.

That was it—I exploded at my dad.

"I come home every day from school and spend two hours cleaning up and washing dishes and clothes and Julius doesn't do anything except make more dishes and clothes for me to wash!"

I don't resent Julius for it, but he doesn't help. How could my father think of getting Julius a present and leaving the rest of us out?

My dad started to yell, "It's my money. I worked for it. And I'll decide who I buy presents for and who I don't!"

That really set me off. It kept on like that nearly all the way home. Letty was just sitting there, listening to all of this as things got louder and louder. Finally, when we were only a few blocks from home, my dad stopped the car and just glared at me with one of his "don't push me any farther" looks that makes me so nervous. Usually I apologize at this point, but I wasn't going to give in on this. He was being totally unfair, and he knew it.

But then he very quietly ordered me out of "his" car. It's when he stops yelling and gets that quiet tone that you know things have gone too far. So I got out of "his" car. I wasn't going to be foolish; I knew I'd reached his limit. I walked home alone. That's not the safest area for a girl to be walking by herself on a Saturday night. My dad couldn't care less. And I was so mad that I didn't care what happened to me. Anyway, it was his fault, and if I got raped or killed, it would be on his conscience forever. I wonder if it would have bothered him?

By the time I got home, Mom and Dad were teamed up together, and I had to sit through one of those lecture-screams for what seemed like forever. They tried to make me apologize for what I'd said, but I wouldn't. I knew I was right and my father knew I was right, too. They got to yell and they got to blame me and they got in the last words, but I never apologized. Finally, they let me go to bed.

This relationship with my parents seems to be more and more like a boxing match where someone is keeping score of who wins what round and who loses. I don't like it being a competition. Why can't people just talk about things, instead of argue? And why does there have to be a winner and a loser?

I don't understand, but I know from now on if there's going to be a competition, I'm not going to just sit there and take it. I may not always win, but I'm not going to let it get me down. I'll get back at them when they aren't expecting it.

December 20

Well, I'm outta there at last. It wasn't easy, but it's done. Last Saturday, my parents tried to make things harder on us. My dad told us he wasn't going to let us go out anymore without him or Mom. All the yelling started again, only this time Letty did most of the yelling. Of course, my parents yelled back. I don't think they like the yelling, but I know they like showing us they have control over our lives.

My parents didn't know what to make of the reaction from me. I didn't yell or complain or even slam my door. I think it surprised them. I usually do most of the yelling and Letty is mostly quiet, though she's getting into it more lately. Anyway, I think they didn't know what to do. I guess they decided it would be best to let things cool off, so they said they were going to the market. That's what they always say when they want an excuse to get out of there. I was just glad to have them gone. I went to my room and calmly packed up some of my things. Then I borrowed money from Letty (I can never save any money, but Letty always seems to have some) and left the house, too. Only I didn't go to the market. I just started walking.

I know that parents are supposed to have control over their kids and I know that the kids are supposed to respect that authority, but it had gone too far. I just decided that I wasn't going to put up with it anymore. I felt so calm and so free, because for the first time in my life I knew I was right. Even though I didn't know where I was going, I had the confidence of making a right decision. I was so relaxed and at ease. It's hard to describe, but it felt great. After I had walked around for a while, I went to a phone booth and called my cousin in East L.A. and told her I was moving out. She invited me to stay with her. Not only that, she said she'd come pick me up. So the whole thing worked out with no hassles. I never thought about running away. If I had thought about it, I never would have imagined it to be so simple and so hassle-free.

Obviously, I wasn't there when my parents got home, but Letty told me they couldn't believe it. It really got to my dad, because I hadn't even been upset. He couldn't believe I'd just walk out without stomping around or threatening to leave or anything else. I was more in control of my life than I had ever been before, and it sounded like he knew it too. David would be proud of what I've done. Maybe he'd be able to see the new confidence I have and the new control over my future—well, over my near future. At least I didn't lose my temper, and at least I didn't go to a bus station or something stupid like you see in the movies.

I've been at my cousin's for four days now. Letty is the only person in El Monte who knows where I am staying. I've done everything that I could to fix things up except visit my family. My father just pushed me too far this time. I may never visit them again and he'd deserve it.

First, I went to school to see my counselor and try to explain to him what happened, and he sounded like he understood. He tried to be helpful, but the main thing on his mind was getting me back into school. He listened to my story and sounded sympathetic, but you can tell when a person is just trying to be sincere. It was okay, until I told him I was not going to go home again, no matter what. I said I'd taken enough from my parents and they weren't going to hurt me anymore. His voice changed and he got all authority-like. He told me he was going to have to inform my parents that I'd come in to see him.

That didn't bother me too much because I knew it would have to happen some time. I couldn't go on not attending any school. I hoped maybe my counselor might just check me out of that school and get me into one near my cousin's house. It's funny, for some reason going to school and graduating are so important to me now.

The problem was: my counselor didn't just tell my parents about me. He called them in to school and told them everything I'd said. I thought he was supposed to be my counselor, not my parents'. He said things I never thought they would hear. Letty said my parents were really upset when they left the school. I think my parents have always pretended that our household was perfect. At least they pretended it to the outside world. It was always kind of like we were on stage and my parents were showing us off to the world. Now the truth was known, or at least part of it, and my parents were crushed because the image of the perfect family no longer existed.

Letty said that my parents were between tears and anger all night and that they tried to get Letty to tell them where I was, but she pretended not to know. Letty is more like a best friend than just my little sister. She keeps me posted on what's going on at home and at school so that I know what to do. She called me from the school every day after the last bell. Now that they're out for Christmas vacation, it's more difficult for her to find a way to call.

Before I left, I gave her a note to give to Mr. Healy. Letty has him first period for Algebra, so I knew she could get it to him without any hassles. The only problem is: she forgot to give it to him before school let out for Christmas vacation and now he won't get it until the start of school after New Year's. I don't know where I'll be by then.

Today Letty told me that my father contacted the police to search for me. She said he told the police he knows that everyone in the United States who is under age has to go to school and he doesn't want me breaking the law. As if he cared.

Anyhow, the under age stuff is right in the United States. I know my counselor won't check me out of Mountain View without my parents' signature. So I've pretty much made up my mind to take a bus to my grandparents in Guadalajara. They told me I was always welcome there, and it's the only place I can think of that would be acceptable for my parents and everyone. I know it will crush the image of the "perfect" family for my grandparents, but it's time they knew what was really going on. I think they probably already know. My grandfather is such a gentle, caring man; I can't see him being judgmental, even if he does already know the truth. It's always been hard to hide things from my grandmother. I bet she's always been able to tell what's going on.

There is so much uncertainty in my future and it seems like I should be so upset and off-balance, but this is one of the most in-balance and controlled times I've ever had. No matter what happens in my future, I think I'll be able to handle it.

Chapter 13

ᘒ᙭

Chris?
(Chip's thoughts—January 5)

Toral oday was the first day after Christmas vacation, which in some ways is as hard as the first day in September. The two weeks off have allowed a teacher's mind the luxury of forgetting so much, including the names of half the faces that come through the door. As a way of circumventing that problem, I planned to create new seating charts for each of my classes. As the kids came in I was passing out cards, which eliminated the awkward, "Hi, what's-your-name." And then when I called their names and put them down in the new chart I would automatically have a name to go with each face on the chart.

It wasn't a bad idea. I was busy ensuring that each student had a card when he or she entered. The side conversations were eliminated, as planned. The kids accepted it just as a matter of course because we change the seating chart every two weeks. I think I ought to use this procedure after every major vacation.

The only glitch came during my first-period class, when someone handed me a note. I didn't see who gave it to me; I was busy passing out cards. I just folded the note and put it in my pocket for later. When I did get around to reading the message during lunch, it wasn't at all what I had expected. The note read:

Mr. Healy,

You know (probably) by now that I don't live here in El Monte anymore 'cause I ran away from my house. Hopefully in the future I'll explain to you why.

Right now though I want to congratulate you in your achievements in our geometry class. You're really creating some miracles in there. Keep up the good work.

I'll miss you.

Chris

The note really affected me. I was sad that Chris was gone, worried about her safety, glowing from what she had written, and embarrassed. I felt very special that at a time of such upheaval and displacement in her life, she still felt that it was important to write me the note. But I was embarrassed, for not only did I not remember who had given me the note, I didn't even recognize who this Chris was. I wasn't even sure if Chris was male or female. It's been nearly a full semester and you'd think I would know everyone by this time, even if it is just after Christmas vacation.

As it turns out, I did know who Chris was, but until I got the note I had no idea that she went by the name "Chris." I'd always called her "Christina," and she had seemed happy about that. I have to remember to ask students what name they want me to call them. I try to do that, but I forget things if something like this doesn't happen every once in a while to remind me.

Not only did I discover who Chris is, but I also found out that Letty in my first-period algebra class is her sister. I try not to make family connections unless the students bring it up. I've been told by many students how they hate people asking, "Isn't so-and-so your brother?" I guard against that. I try not to relate to a person by family, but as an individual; I think that's best for everyone. But sometimes it leads to confusion, as in the case of Chris and Letty.

At first in my No Book geometry class Chris was a noninvolved student. She just sat there and looked like she was going to let this experience pass her by—until she finally felt strongly enough about something that she got involved. In Chris's case that something was the definition of the word distance.

The majority of the class felt that the definition of distance was "the space between two points," but Chris was adamant that it was "the space between two or more points." This may not seem like such a big difference, but to Chris, for whatever reason, it was extremely significant. She was ready to argue it, and not just from her seat. She went up to the board, drew pictures, and took on anyone until the class in general decided she must have a point or she wouldn't be so committed. It was not that big a thing to the class, but to Chris it was a turning point that affected the way she approached the entire experience. It gave her involvement, confidence, a positive interaction, and a feeling of belonging.

But if she had a real feeling of belonging, why did she run away? The note said I'd probably know why, but I certainly don't. Did it have to do with my No Book class? Was I in some way responsible for this? Why else would she have written me a note at that time, if I weren't partly to blame?

Wait a minute, I think I'm getting a little paranoid here. This class isn't anything that is going to cause that sort of thing. But why did Chris take the time to write me? Whatever her reason, what she wrote is solid proof that this class is making progress and that it is having an impact on the lives of some of the people in it.

But why do I find out about these things from people who are no longer in the class? Why don't I know each of the students better so that at least I know their correct names? The large class size (it's up to thirty-two now) is no excuse. I think I've been so uptight about the everyday success of the class that I forgot to get to know the people. And they are a very special group of young people. They are willing to try this experiment and have put one-hundred percent of their effort into it.

I think this may turn out to be more than just a new way for a group of students to look at the subject of geometry. In fact, it appears that with this method they will learn a great deal not only about geometry, but about life as well. About taking a stand, as Chris did with the definition of distance. About communicating, as Patty did with her pictures of parallel lines intersected by a third line.

Good things are happening all the time in the class. I'm too involved in day-to-day events and all the extraneous demands on my time to be able to see it. But if Chris can take time to write when her life appears to be coming down around her, things must be working.

When I got home from school today, I found a pigeon on the steps. It seemed happy to be there and didn't seem bothered by me. My daughters and I made a home for it in a box and brought it in. We thought it might be hurt, so we decided to keep it for a while and take care of it. I didn't tell my girls why, but I suggested we name it Chris. I hope someone takes her in while she is hurting and cares for her. My daughters liked the name, so I think it'll stick. I don't have any idea how to take care of a pigeon, but I guess we'll find out.

Chris's note has given me a different perspective on the No Book class. I'm really beginning to believe that this class may be a significant stop on the road to success for the students. I've always wanted to help each individual develop as a person as well as learn the subject matter I taught. This class seems like it's going to be just what I want in teaching. Chris may never know what she did by taking the time to write me that simple little note and getting her sister to deliver it.

After I put the girls to bed, I went in to the computer and wrote Chris the following note.

Dear Chris,

Letty gave me the note you wrote. It was super to hear from you, and what you said about me "creating some miracles" in the geometry class made me feel really good. A lot of great things have happened to me regarding that geometry class, but what you said in your note was the best of all. The reason you think I am able to do miracles with that class is that I was lucky enough to be given some people who are miracles. You are one of those people. You're a special person.

I'll miss you and all the things you brought to class— your enthusiasm, your energy, your smile, and the courage to let others know how you felt. But that's not nearly as important as your life in El Monte being over.

What happened at home to force you to leave? I asked Letty, but she didn't seem to want to say anything—I figured she was just not sure what to tell me. You're lucky to have her as your sister. If you don't want to explain, I'll understand. But it seems unfair to me that such a special person had to make a decision to leave her home. If I can help, let me know.

Things are going well in your old geometry class. There are a number of articles in magazines and newspapers mentioning it, a videotape, and more and more people all over interested in what is happening in fifth period. If all the things that have been said come true, it will be an interesting second semester.

If things ever settle down and you can return, there will always be a place waiting for you in fifth period. Take care of yourself—you are an important person.

Mr. Healy

Chapter 14

ૐ·

Pythagoras—Park Style
(Edmund's thoughts—January 21)
(Chip's thoughts—January 22)

I still don't see what the big deal is. A couple of weeks ago I figured out a way to get the same results as the Pythagorean Theorem using an isosceles right triangle (a triangle with a 90-degree angle and two sides the same length). I did it by folding the paper and it worked out fine. But no one cares if you have a proof of something for only one isolated case. When I showed it to Mr. Healy, he said the same thing. He seemed impressed and told me to keep working on it, though, so I did.

I found out it works for some other right triangles. When I showed it to Mr. Healy this time, he was really excited. He asked me to present it to the rest of the class, using the board to demonstrate it. I'm not exactly a public speaker, but I wanted the rest of the class to see it, and I knew Mr. Healy wouldn't show it to them—that's just the way he is.

Today was the day for my presentation. I had it all planned on graph paper, but I was pretty sure that most of the class wouldn't even care about what I'd done. I just didn't want them to make fun of me. I still don't speak English very well. I know how to read and write it well, but presenting this to a class of people like Larry and the others could have been real embarrassing. So I had it as organized as I could. I thought if things were well planned, people would give me more of a chance before they told me to sit down. When I went up to do the presentation, I was organized and ready for the class to hassle me.

But I froze. I didn't completely stop, but I got so nervous that I lost my notes—or they got disassembled. Anyway, the presentation was a disaster. I got the picture up on the board and I even showed them why it works, but they didn't understand. I don't know if it was because my English is so poor or if I just didn't present it right. When I finally got to the end of my notes, the class was lost and I knew it. All through the presentation they just sat there. It's not that they aren't smart, I just couldn't present it right. I was up there for nearly half the period, until Mr. Healy finally interrupted. I was so grateful he rescued me from my disastrous presentation. My gratitude didn't last very long, because Mr. Healy thanked me and then asked the class if they would like to have me explain it again!

Everyone voted for me to go over it again. This time I didn't even try to use my notes, and it seemed to go better. I still had trouble explaining it, but this time a couple of the people in the class asked questions and I guess that helped everybody. It seemed like I'd been up there the whole period when Mr. Healy finally rescued me for real.

He thanked me, as if I'd done a good job. Then he asked how many students really understood what I'd presented. Only seven people raised their hands. He didn't stop there, though. Next, he asked how many felt that they kind of understood. There were nine of those. The ultimate embarrassment, he asked how many didn't under-stand at all. Eight people raised their hands. I'm glad I got through to at least some of them. But I know when a good teacher really understands what he is talking about, he gets through to everyone.

I know what I am talking about because this is my proof. I didn't get it from anywhere else, so I have no excuses for not communicating with everyone. I know a third of the class understanding is much better than nobody, but that means I missed getting the idea across to two-thirds of the people. But at least the presentation wasn't as bad an experience as I thought it would be.

I think my presentation went better than Larry's did on the Metric Circle. Usually Larry knows how to get his ideas across, but I can't do it. People just listen better to Larry. I guess they think more like he does. The others are smart, they just don't think like I do.

It seems like I am beyond where most of the others think, so the class is getting boring for me. I can still come up with new things like my Pythagorean Proof, but I want to be able to think with the others, and they aren't on the same level that I am on. I put in about two hours every night thinking about geometry and all the possibilities—I don't think the others are doing that. How can they expect to get all there is out of a class like this if they aren't willing to put in the time?

One thing that happened today I don't understand. It has to do with how I think and who I am.

After my explanation, Larry said, "This Edmund dude thinks in the fifth dimension." He also said that the rest of the class is still thinking in the third dimension. I don't quite understand what Larry is saying about me when he says I think in the fifth dimension. But, I was glad to have Larry say anything about me. I know he's the leader in the class. If he noticed me, then I know I must be making progress, even if it is in the fifth dimension.

Sergio said, "If he's going to be thinking in the fifth dimension, we need an interpreter to understand him."

I'd rather they had to have an interpreter to get me in the right dimension than a translator to make my English understandable. Maybe I'd get along better in the class if I learned how to speak in their dimension. I should be able to think on both levels, so I'm going to work on finding out how to speak to them in their dimension. Maybe Larry would be willing to help me.

Here's what I presented to the class today in the order that I had planned to present it. I had a little help from Alicia, who volunteered to draw the picture on the board for me.

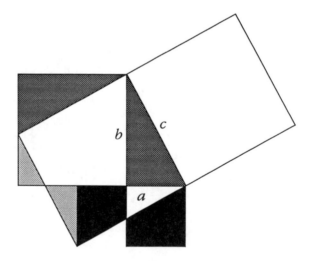

The original triangle is the right triangle in the middle with sides a, b, and c. I then drew the squares on each side to represent a squared, b squared, and c squared. Next you need to take the square on side c and fold it back over the original triangle. This will give you the picture I have shown above. You can easily see that the areas of the smaller squares add up to the area of the large square.

The white areas are areas that are part of the smaller squares that are covered by the square.

The vertically striped triangle of square *b* fits on the vertically striped triangle on square *c*.

The dotted areas match up, as do the slanted striped areas.

The result is the area of the *a* square plus the area of the *b* square is equal to the area of the *c* square.

It's not exactly Euclid, but it does work.

Chip's thoughts—January 22

Yesterday was a teacher's dream presentation of the Pythagorean Theorem. Only in this case, the teacher was an observer, not the presenter. Edmund Park had the entire class totally absorbed in the concept of the Pythagorean Theorem. For half the period there wasn't a sound from the entire class because they were so involved in trying to understand his proof. After he had completed his presentation, I interrupted and asked if the class would like to have it presented to them again. Every single student raised his or her hand. What a difference from when I presented this material in years past!

For the repeat presentation I asked Alicia to draw the figure more clearly on the board—Edmund is a great thinker and creator, but his illustrations leave something to be desired. With the new picture and the first explanation behind him, Edmund began again with more confidence. This time he was stopped repeatedly by questions from students trying to grasp what he was saying. They asked him to slow down or repeat parts of the proof. Whether or not they were learning was not readily apparent, but they were definitely involved in trying to learn and wanted to understand. Why can't all teaching be like this?

As far as Edmund's proof is concerned, I am extremely impressed. Some high school math teachers may know how many proofs there are of the Pythagorean Theorem and may be familiar with most of them, but that isn't so for me. I am aware of a half dozen or so and I'm sure there must be more somewhere. So the possibility exists that Edmund's proof isn't a discovery for the world, but I haven't seen it before. He first showed it to me a few weeks ago, when he could only make it work for isosceles right triangles. So I did see the derivation of the proof, and I believe it is sound and unique. I suppose the possibility exists that Edmund is a genius and I just happened to have him in the No Book class, but I think it's more likely that he is bright and hard working and flourishes in the environment of discovery in the class.

Chapter 15

è▲·

The First Semester Ends
(Carmen's thoughts—January 28)
(Larry's thoughts—January 29)
(Chip's thoughts—February 1)

Carmen's thoughts

It was terrible. I just know I flunked it. I can't do geometry and I certainly can't do the geometry that was on that final. Mr. Healy gave us a final from the book they used last year and we aren't using that book. In fact the only "book" we are using changes whenever the class wants it to. Every couple of weeks we get a new "edition" with all the new stuff we've discovered or defined—plus all the old stuff with changes, if we decided to make any. It's so confusing. And then he expects us to take a final from a book we've never even seen before.

I talked to a bunch of people in the class, and they all thought it was hard. Well, all of them except for Larry, who would never admit anything was too hard. But even Edmund said it wasn't very easy. Alicia's brother is in a geometry class which is using a book and he even said it was a really hard final.

I guess there's more than one geometry. I don't see exactly how that can be, though, because the world is the world, isn't it? So who makes the changes? The guys who write the books?

That would be kind of funny though—if the authors made the changes in the books like we do in our class. Who'd check and see if they were doing it right? There could be lots of errors and maybe no one would notice. But it's got to be something like that, otherwise how would there be differences?

Alicia told me her brother hasn't even heard of "Axioms." Maybe the words we have in our class describe the same things as other geometries, but so far we haven't figured that out yet. Wow, that's strange to think about.

Maybe it's like the book I'm writing—it's over fifteen chapters and even I don't know how it's all going to end. When I write I'm like in another place and things happen and I have no control over them. It's like there's this whole world in my head and there are things actually happening to people who are actually there. All I do is write it down as it happens. I'm sort of like a reporter.

I think it's good for me to get away from everything and experience something just in my mind. Sometimes it's like I'm the main character in my story and living through her. Other times I'm a totally different person just observing and recording what's going on. It's kind of weird. I hope I'm not crazy creating stuff like this. Sometimes I'm really into it and other times I'm really into what is going on around me at school, at home, or wherever I am.

I like writing, no matter what kind of writing I'm doing. I like to get into the life of a character in a story and figure out everything there is to know about that person. Even things which don't matter. And I'm going to use writing to help my geometry grade next semester. I don't think my geometry grade will be very good this semester, but next semester it's going to be better. Last week, Mr. Healy said that in the second semester we'd all have a chance to do a project on anything we wanted as long as there was some kind of connection to math or geometry. I know exactly what I want to do. I want to find a scientist or mathematician and really go into their background, become that person, and write a story from their perspective about the world. Now all I have to do now is find that person. We've got until the end of April to turn it in, so I've got plenty of time.

Larry's thoughts—January 28th

Okay, now what are you gonna do, Healy? You've played with grades long enough, and now you have absolute proof that we aren't learning shit in this class. Of course, I could have told you a long time ago, if you bothered to ask me. The grades on our finals will be so low you won't be able to see them. I figure if it was hard for me, it must have been terrible for the rest of those hopeless creatures.

You say the responsibility is ours in this class and you're not going to give us any input. Well, fella, your little experiment with our minds is over and everyone loses. Only when the scores come out, it will be Healy with most of the shit on his face. The responsibility is his. I knew it would be like this. You can't give responsibility to a bunch of teenagers who don't know which way is up.

This won't stop me. I won't even look back. I'm ready to check out of this class as soon as the next semester gets going. I've talked to my counselor about it and he says I have to wait until after the end of the first week of the second semester. Then he'll move me to another class and I'll be outa there. Poor Enoch and Gerardo, they're going to be stuck in there the rest of the year. Crazy Shawn is just checking in at the start of the second semester. After he wrote that article in the school paper, he thought he wanted to get involved in the class. Since he failed the second semester of geometry last year, he thought he'd be in this class with me. Well, surprise, I won't be there.

I don't know what Healy'll do with the others in the class, especially the ones who need to learn real geometry for their SAT tests and stuff, but that's his problem.

The Metric Circle may not have caught on while I was in this class, but wait till I've made my money in real estate. I'll use my money and my influence to help the world find an easier solution to the 360-degree circle. I think the world would operate a lot more efficiently if the complicated stuff were simplified—like using the Park Proof to explain the Pythagorean Theorem. Edmund's proof is the first explanation I ever understood of why the Pythagorean Theorem works. I know it would take a lot of influence and money, but I'll do that for future suckers like Enoch.

I think I'll get the Park Proof published at one of my book-publishing places. I'll get Alicia to be in charge of that end of things; she's good at organizing and you need that to make a good book. I'll need a few people who know how to work with the public for PR work. Carmen, Sergio, and Enoch know how to handle people. I can use them to build my empire. I'll put Edmund in a think tank to come up with ideas, which I'll convert from the fifth dimension into language everyone can understand. We'll make a fortune.

I can see it all now. Geometry Camp in the summer instead of Band Camp. There'd be no rules, you could think about anything. If anyone came up with any great ideas, we could market them right then and there. And why stop there, we could have Algebra Camp, Trigonometry Camp, Calculus Camp, and who knows what else.

Hold it. This thing is getting out of hand here. The No Book experiment is about to dissolve and here I am planning all this shit about a nonexistent class. What's going on here? That class must have rotted my mind or something, but now it's over. For the others, it's still a geometry class. For me it's history.

Chip's thoughts—February 2

I don't know whether to be happy or sad about the results of the first semester finals. To begin with, my algebra class and my basic math classes did great. They were the highest in the school in their categories and so things are going well in those classes. But I really hoped the No Book class would show their knowledge on the geometry final. I know they aren't studying the same course, they aren't covering it in the same order, and their vocabulary is different, but I was hoping we'd do so much better.

The first results looked very bad for the No Book class; their average was twelve percent below the regular geometry class I taught. At that point I was ready to throw in the towel. Ken was wrong—the kids could be worse off than in a regular geometry class.

However, when I got the results from Yvette's geometry classes, the No Book class average was only five percent lower. That's more reasonable.

Of course, it could be that my other geometry class is the brightest of the four geometry classes at Mountain View. Each year there has to be a brightest class, and that could be it, simply by chance. On the other hand, it's also possible that the No Book class is the strongest class and the only reason they are only five percent behind is due to their tremendous potential. Perhaps an average geometry class would have been fifteen percent behind the others.

Just suppose the worst scenario is true. What choice do I have? There are people all over who know about this class, and if that newspaper article in the *Los Angeles Times* becomes a reality, what can I do? I've just got to go through with it. No matter what, all of us have to see it through.

There has been incredible support from all directions. Yvette and Ken, Toby and the PLUS teachers from other math departments, Grace at EDC, and those I met in MSTI last summer, they all believe in the No Book class. They can't all be wrong. They have faith—they must see something really positive for math education coming out of that class.

This isn't an easy situation, but I started it and we have to see it through. Things could be a lot worse. Five percent is not that much, all things considered. In fact, I'm going to stress to the class that the five percent difference is positive evidence that we are making it.

Chapter 16

ẽ☙

Picture This, or
Let Bigons be Bygones
(Alicia's thoughts—February 15)

It was great. A few weeks ago our group was investigating the possible existence of bigons. A bigon is assumed to be a two sided figure. I have my opinion about bigons and I was really into the argument we were having about their existence. I still can't believe we get into such incredible disagreements about things that we couldn't have cared less about last summer. Enoch and I agreed, but Shawn and Patty really disagreed. Sergio was somewhere in between. So I called Mr. Healy over and asked him to draw his idea of a bigon for our group.

You know I used to think he was this person with all this knowledge (I always thought math teachers were probably smarter than everyone else), but he was keeping it from us, like it was some sort of game. When I found out how unorganized he is, I realized he's fallible just like the rest of the world. And now I don't know how smart he is, but it doesn't matter anymore.

Mr. Healy didn't know what he was getting into when I asked him to draw a bigon. I didn't know what he'd draw, but I was sure he wasn't going to agree with what Shawn and Patty said. Well, his picture didn't look like either of ours. We all kind of jumped on his case when he drew his picture of a bigon.

It's funny how the class went from believing Mr. Healy was the basis of knowledge for geometry, begging him for answers, to the point now, where no matter what he says, we don't feel any obligation to agree with him. That day, the *Los Angeles Times*, which was doing some sort of article about schools, needed some pictures of a classroom, and for some reason they chose ours. So they were there and took dozens of pictures during that class.

Well, it turned out the article they were doing was about the No Book class. Some of the pictures they took were going to be used to go along with the article. They used two pictures, including the one that was taken of our group just after we had gotten on Mr. Healy's case for drawing such a stupid picture of a bigon. So next to the article, there's Mr. Healy trying to explain why his drawing of a bigon makes sense, and snap! they take the picture. Most of the people who read the article don't have any idea why he has such a funny look on his face, but the people in our group know exactly why. I think that's one of the things I'll always remember about this class.

Here we were discussing bigons, something I'd never heard of before (and something I know isn't in my brother's regular geometry book) and getting on a teacher's case for his own opinion. Boy, this sure isn't what I expected to be doing in geometry. The existence of bigons or anygons were supposed to be things we were told about. But not in this class. That makes this class especially hard for me.

I think I have a photogenic memory. All I need to do is read a book once and I can pretty much tell you what is on any page. If you give me a book and let me read a page, then take the book away, I store the information. Later, if I want to know what's on that page, I just close my eyes and sort of look on the inside of my forehead (this sounds really bizarre, but it's how I work). It's like I have a monitor inside my forehead. I put on the video and just read down the page to the part I need. I'm not sure if other people can do this or if I'm really weird, but I know it works for me.

If the information I need is in a book I've read, I sort of put the video of the whole book up there. Then I just scan each page until I find the information I'm looking for.

It's always been really helpful for tests and assignments, but in that geometry class it's almost an anti-help. Each time we get a new edition of the book to study for a test I have to read it so I can picture it. But we change things in each edition. Sometimes when my brain gets a videobook out, I think I get the wrong edition. I can get really confused. We have to keep up with all the changes if we're going to make it in this class, that's why I keep notes. That's also why Mr. Healy can always depend on me for the notes of things we agree on.

You know, I think my brain is a lot like a computer in the way it remembers things. The more I learn about computers, the more I think I'm really like that. I wonder if the people who developed the computer had a photogenic memory like mine? I'm using Appleworks to remember the information from the geometry class. The more I learn, the more I see the similarity between human memory and computer memory. I think I have video data disks in my brain where I store information.

The only problem with my video data disk is that I have to do all the reading to make sure I input all the information, but I almost always get straight A's. Alex, my brother, doesn't work nearly as hard to input the information. He says he just listens in class and then figures out what the teacher is going to ask and then he just reviews that stuff for the tests. His grades aren't quite as high as mine, but he doesn't spend the time I do inputting everything.

My grades in the geometry class get messed up in two ways: (1) The book changes from edition to edition (we've changed the definition of "rectangle" five times); (2) Mr. Healy's tests.

The day before a test the new "edition" (actually it's a computer printout that he dittoed and I stapled) comes out. We spend that day going over the book and finding any errors or changes that need to be made.

It usually works, but Mr. Healy gave us the first test of the second semester only three days after we'd finished the first semester final, which was unbelievably difficult. The day we were supposed to go over the latest edition, the whole class was kicking back talking to each other. We weren't ready for any more testing. Mr. Healy tried to lead the discussion about changes, but we ignored him and sat there talking. Hey, everyone needs a day off once in a while, even me. Besides, last-minute changes in our book are one of the things I like least about this class. When Mr. Healy figured out we weren't interested, he just walked over to his desk and sat down. You know, that's still one of the hardest things for me to accept about Mr. Healy. He doesn't force us to learn.

A few of us waited for him to try again, but he didn't. When he finally did go over to the podium, instead of stopping to talk, he picked up some papers and just kept going. He went out the door and disappeared.

We were sitting there and he was gone. I don't know what went on in the other groups, but our group figured we better come up with something about the book. That way when he did come back, we would look like we were really doing something.

Then Larry took over, "Hey, remember what Healy did to us on the last test? We can't let him get away with that again. For example, on page eight there's a typo, it says 'angels' when it should be 'angles.' If we don't fix that that he'll ask us about wings and halos."

Just after that, Mr. Healy walked in. We all expected him to take over now, so Larry went to sit down. Surprise! Mr. Healy walked straight over to his desk, picked up some more papers, and just walked right back out of the room.

So Larry walked right back up to the podium and continued. By that time no one knew what to think, but we all got really into the discussion and changes in the book and I think we accomplished more that day than ever before. I know I felt the best I ever had about our book. I felt I had a better chance on the next test than on any of the others.

You see, Mr. Healy has this thing about tests. He says he is like Dr. Jekyl in the daytime, but the night before our tests he becomes Mr. Hyde to write up the most fiendish tests possible. Mr. Healy jokes about the Jekyl/Hyde change, but I'm not so sure it's really a joke. It's true that in the daytime he's really nice. And it's also true that he makes the hardest tests I've ever taken.

Each test is divided into three sections:

1. *Sometimes, Always, Never.* It's like True/False only harder, because you have to determine if the statement is sometimes true, always true, or never true, and it all has to be according to our book.

2. *Fill in the Blanks.* It's so difficult because our book changes and there are errors.

3. *Validations*. This is the easiest part and my brother does these, only he calls them proofs.

It may not sound difficult, but the first two parts are so confusing. You've got to really know the book, but even then it's almost impossible to get an A or B. Here are a few of the questions from the last test before the semester final that I'll never forget. The correct answers are in parentheses below:

Sometimes, Always, Never

10._____ Space is area.

11._____ The endpoints of a line are congruent.

12._____ Lines are always straight.

13._____ A line segment in a hexagon that was drawn from the center of one side to the center of another side is parallel to one side.

14._____ A point has no length or width so it is invisible.

15._____ Any two angles in a parallelogram are either congruent or supplementary.

10. (S) 11. (S) 12. (A) 13. (A) 14. (S) 15. (A)

Fill in the Blanks

32._____ A statement that can be validated with logical reasoning.

33._____ =

34._____ Parallel lines intersected by a third line.

35._____ _____ are angles that add up to 90 degrees.

32. (Proven Fact)   33. (Circumference)   34. (Parasector)

35. (Complimentary Angles)

These are questions from the January test. We fixed most of the errors. We made space a 3-D vocabulary word, made all points congruent, put in definitions for circumference and complementary angles (and changed the spelling of complementary). If I know Mr.

Healy, he'll find more, but on the test that Larry reviewed us for, I got an A—92%. That was my first A on a test in this class.

The day after we went over the tests, the actual article appeared in the *L.A. Times*, including the bigons picture of Mr. Healy. The article was about the class and about Edmund's proof, which we call the Park Proof now. It said we had a unique class and that learning was really taking place in the class. I definitely agree that it is a unique class and I know some kind of learning is going on. I'm not sure it's geometry learning, but on the first semester final I got almost the same score as my brother, and his class has a book.

The article also had quotes in it from Mr. Healy, a professor at the University of Wisconsin, and Toby, the lady in charge of PLUS, but the best one was from Carmen in our class. She said, "I like the class because we use our imagination, not [only] our brains." I guess the class is special and we are doing something unique. You know, if Carmen, who's not doing well at all, thinks it's great, maybe it is.

Still, to me it's just a class I take with a teacher who's a nice, disorganized guy where all the rules (like teachers not leaving the room) are changeable.

Oh, and by the way, even though the topic of bigons was a big thing, like so many other things my groups have been involved in, nothing ever became of the idea. Except that goofy picture of Mr. Healy that appeared in the newspaper. After four days of investigation, discussion, *Supposer* demonstrations, and debate, our group decided to let bigons be bygones.

Chapter 17

è.

Who Are These Guys?
(Chip's thoughts—February 21-23)

I made it to the weekend, but this has to have been the most unpredictable No Book week ever, except maybe for that first week. The class has sparked interest from many places. The PLUS project is one of those places. After they found out about it they asked me if they could arrange a class visit for teachers from other schools. When the project leader, Toby, asked me about it a couple of months ago, I was flattered. So I agreed, but it wasn't until last weekend that I began to realize the consequences of having visitors in class. I remember the way I felt Tuesday.

Tuesday evening, February 20

I can't "prepare a special lesson" to present to the students on Thursday's visit because the students create their own lessons for each day. This really has worked out fine so far, but now that there will be others watching…I don't know how I feel. How will others from outside the environment of the class react to the idea? What attitudes about math and the curriculum are they bringing to my classroom?

They could disrupt the unique environment. And they probably know so much more math than I do. What will I do if they ask a bunch of questions I can't answer?

It's less than forty-eight hours away and I have no control of the curriculum the visitors will observe. Oh well, regardless of what happens, I can't change strategies in the middle of the course just for these unknown people. They'll see what they see, whether it's utopia or anarchy. Now to the business at hand.

Group One has been looking into the idea of dimensions beyond the third and has some fascinating thoughts about the fourth dimension. Most of us assume the experts somehow know that the fourth dimension is time and leave it at that. Group One doesn't see it that way. They were trying to get the fourth dimension out of the third dimension. Their logic says that each dimension is derived from the addition of a perpendicular line. Following this logic, they spent the whole time in class today discussing it and trying to get another perpendicular, but couldn't construct it.

One of the most interesting statements on their investigation sheet is in the reverse direction. Their idea of the zero dimension is determined by subtracting a perpendicular from the first dimension, which is a straight line in their terminology. They are working so well together and are so invested in this topic that I think I will use that statement about the zero dimension for their next investigation sheet.

Tomorrow's topic for Group Two came from the sheet done by Group Six. Group Six had been investigating what they call "perfect" shapes. I think that's a regular shape, but I'm not sure if their undefined term means the same thing. If I can find another word or two I can assign "perfect shape" for homework tomorrow night. Anyway, they said, "A perfect shape with an infinite number of sides is a circle." Group Two will get that statement.

Group Three has requested to use the *Supposer* tomorrow. They are looking for the center of shapes and objects. That's a difficult concept. I'm not sure that the *Supposer* can handle this one, but they can try. Who knows?

Group Four doesn't want me to know what they are doing. They are kind of secretive about things and want to do a presentation on their findings on Friday. It has to do with one of the Given Truths—parallel lines never meet. But their paper today was nearly blank. It had only the request to continue for two more days to prepare their "discovery." I'm not sure they know what they are doing, and they've got Bernie, an artist who used to drive Larry crazy with the different way he sees. Larry is in that group, so whatever they present Friday will be most interesting.

I'll give Group Five their topic for tomorrow from the sheet of the Group Six. It is on the angles of "proportional" shapes (another homework definition for tomorrow). The statement I picked says, "The angles in proportional shapes are equal." Does this mean "proportional shapes" are similar shapes or regular shapes? Maybe they are regular, similar shapes. Could be anything. I mentioned on their sheet that the computer is being used by Group Three, but that they can request it for later in the day if the other group gets finished.

Group Six is going to have an interesting time. I took a statement off the sheet of Group Two about earthquake-proof bricks. I wasn't involved in the discussion, so I don't know what went on. Group Two was supposed to be investigating the statement, "A parabola (pronounced par-a-bol'-a in this class) is half an oval." Clearly they didn't look at that statement much, but this earthquake-proof bricks idea is a good one for Group Six.

Group Seven has been working on measuring degrees and Group Six, the group working on perfect shapes, has a statement on its investigation sheet about measuring an angle made by a straight line and an arc. Let's see what Group Seven will do with this one.

Group Eight spent practically the whole period today in the faculty men's rest room. They stayed long after class working on their theory about reflections. I opened the door for them and went and got the flashlight they requested, but mostly I left them alone until after class. If the student rest rooms at our school didn't have so much graffiti and vandalism that all the mirrors had to be removed, Group Eight could have been in the student rest rooms and not the faculty rest room. But it was funny to see all four of the members of Group Eight jammed into the tiny rest room used by the men teachers in our building. I think Patty is doing something about non-coplanar lines, but I don't know. They requested to continue tomorrow on their sheet, so that's what I'll let them do. I've gotten much more relaxed about them continuing an investigation for more than a day.

Wednesday evening, February 21

Tomorrow's the day the teachers come in to visit. I wish it had been today. If today's No Book class could have been videotaped and shown to everyone, it would have looked perfect. I know the class doesn't always go smoothly, but today was a concert of engaged, enthusiastic groups of students. But tomorrow anything can happen. Oh, why wasn't the visit scheduled a day earlier?

In class I made no mention of tomorrow's visitors. I'm not sure that's right, but what's done is done. It's class as usual as far as the students know. My preparation will be done with that in mind.

Group One is really into this dimension thing. On their sheet today they speculated that if the fourth dimension were time and if you could time travel, the way to reverse the travel and return to the present would be through the negative fourth dimension. That's what

I am going to put for their topic tomorrow and I'll ask them to prepare a presentation for Friday.

Group Two worked on the circles today but could not come up with a way of proving or disproving that they had very short straight sides. For tomorrow I am going to have them investigate measuring degrees in an arc, which is what Group Seven wrote about.

Group Three spent the day on the computer, first praising and then cursing at the *Supposer.* There is no place on that machine that just says "center." Maybe shapes don't have centers. What is a center, anyway? That sounds like a word needing a definition, if the students ask for it. Group Three decided that they find out more by folding waxed paper than by using the computer, so they are bringing some to class tomorrow for further investigation into the topic of centers.

Group Four dropped the bombshell on me this afternoon after class. They all stayed and missed most of their next class to explain to me that all parallel lines meet. There was much talking and arguing and demonstrating, but I still doubted they had uncovered much. Then Bernie said he'd bring a basketball tomorrow and show it to the entire group, and he wanted me to be in the group to see. I don't understand what they are trying to do. I think it all may be a charade to challenge one of the Given Truths for the sake of the challenge, but I honestly don't know.

Group Five streamlined their investigation sheet statement today. It now reads: "Angles that are in the same place in proportional shapes are equal." They didn't get a chance on the computer today, but I'll let them have the computer first tomorrow.

Group Six will get a statement from the investigation sheet of Group Three. The statement is: "If there are short straight sides on a circle, then the angles between the sides are 1 degree each and there are 360 sides." This should be a good one for Group Six.

Group Seven will have a shot at the earthquake problem. Today Group Six drew several different shapes that they could try as earthquake-proof bricks. I'm sure each model pictured had some reasoning behind its design, but that logic was missing from most of the pictures. Clearly the most popular design was some interlocking bricks. The logic with that design was included: "These bricks would let the building sort of move and not really, so the building wouldn't collapse." However reasonable this idea, the group conclusion was that the problem needed to be looked at for an entire building, not just single bricks. So tomorrow I'll let Group Seven look at what Group Six calls earthquake-proof buildings.

Group Eight discovered a mirror in the closet in the back of my room and asked me if they could scrape off some of the reflective stuff on the back so they could see through some of it. That mirror has been there forever and is never used, so why not? They were working on it as the bell rang. More on reflections tomorrow for this group.

That's the way this class ends too frequently: with groups still trying to get through their investigations. When the bell rang today, with everyone trying to get a few more minutes out of class time to work on their investigation sheets, there I was assigning homework. The homework was to create definitions for perfect shape, dimension, and proportional shape. Oh no! I didn't reserve a group to determine the class definition of the words. Organization is definitely not my thing. I think I'll give it to Group Six and have them do that first, and if they get done I'll give them the topic on angles in a circle.

Ready or not, visitors from other classrooms come tomorrow.

Thursday afternoon, February 22

This morning before school Bernie arrived in my classroom with a basketball and masking tape and asked if he could store them in my room for the day. This has gotten to be more the norm than the exception, and I have cleared out two big shelves in the cupboard in back just for No Book miscellany. (Appropriately enough, the space used to be used to store geometry books.) Bernie shoved the Park Proof information and manipulatives further back on the shelf, along with some large sheets of cardboard with pictures on them extolling the merits of the Metric Circle, and other things. In went the basketball and the tape and out the door went Bernie to his first-period class.

The day went by slowly for me as I awaited my No Book class and our visitors. My fourth-period class is a general math class. I hadn't thought about it, but somehow I guess I had imagined that the visitors would arrive exactly at the start of fifth period. Surprise, they got there early. Double surprise, when they knocked on the door I was standing on a desk in the middle of the class, reviewing fractions. It hadn't dawned on me that this interruption would mean visitors. Oops again.

I watched out of the corner of my eye as the eight teachers and Toby from PLUS entered my class and stood against the wall. Their introduction to the No Book teacher did nothing to assure them that this guy wasn't some kind of freak. This was the first day I had ever stood on a desk in my class, but when it happened, it woke the students up and they were more intent on solving fraction problems than ever before. I'm not sure I'll use this particular technique again, but whatever works...

The class ended soon after, and I just had enough time to say "Hi" to Toby and thank her for coming before the No Book people started to come in. (They tend to arrive early.) I grabbed one of them and asked him to stand at the door and collect the assignments. At the beginning of the year I always collected the homework myself, but then students started volunteering. They do a fine job, so now either a student volunteers or I ask one of them to collect homework.

While the homework was being collected, I explained to the visitors—four men and five women—that there are no rules and they are free to wander, ask questions, make comments, offer advice, or just stand and observe. I did a quick mental survey of each of their reactions to the class, which may or may not have been influenced by the standing-on-the-desk incident. Two of the men, one younger and one older, seemed to be withholding any interest in the class. The only verbal reaction I had was from Barbara, who came from a school in south Los Angeles. She asked if I always conducted class from atop a desk in the center of the room. I had the momentary impulse to say yes, but I chose honesty instead and said, "I use anything that works."

The No Book class began as usual. The students were seated and talking about teenage topics. When I was ready to proceed with the class, I stood at the podium and hit it twice, which has become the signal to get started. I acknowledged the visitors and again told them they were free to walk around and take part in the class. Then I reiterated to the students that this is their classroom and they control what happens in here.

The order of day followed the normal routine from there. I went over some of the exciting things going on, such as Group Eight's work on the reflections and the see-through reflections of the mirror in the closet; Group One's discussion on the existence of a negative fourth dimension; and of course I mentioned that Group Four was preparing a bombshell to blow one of the Given Truths out of existence. Then I poured my daily dose of positive support, reminding the students that they were doing magnificent things and discovering things that no one else in the world knew.

Before handing out the investigation sheets, I announced that Group Five would get to use the computer first today. Then I passed out the investigation sheets, gave the homework sheets to Group Six to create a class definition of each word, and helped Bernie get his basketball and masking tape out. One of the members of Group Eight asked me for a screwdriver to remove the mirror from the closet. Next, Group Two asked for chalk and permission to go outside to the basketball courts on the blacktop, which I let them do. Then I talked to Group Seven, who had a problem understanding the picture I had drawn on their investigation sheet of the earthquake-proof brick. So I redrew it and explained that the previous group thought that the secret was not in the construction of the bricks, but in the construction of the entire building.

By the time I had a chance to rest and look at the class as a whole, I found all but one of the visitors involved in watching or participating in a group. The negative fourth dimension discussion caused three visitors to pull up desks and become actively involved in the group. Bernie was demonstrating his reasoning with the basketball and masking tape to his group, which included a nonargumentative Larry. He was as mesmerized as Larry ever gets. Toby had become part of this group as had Greg, the young teacher who had what I thought was a doubting attitude. He seemed to question everything Bernie did, and this seemed to suit Larry just fine.

Ted, who has a whole set of Apple II's in his classroom, was grilling the kids in the group on the *Supposer.* I doubt that he thought he'd observe a class with such opinionated students, but their opinions and evaluation of the *Supposer* were important to him. Plus he had the unique opportunity to see students using the geometry software to investigate conjectures it wasn't designed to investigate. This put him in an excellent position to evaluate the strengths and weaknesses of the program.

Three of the teachers (Espy, Odessa, and Alan) seemed entranced by the possibility of such a class existing. They went from group to group, stopping for a few minutes here and there and asking probing questions of the students. Odessa focused on the mathematics being learned here; she teaches AP Calculus and had a natural interest. Espy had read about the class in the *Los Angeles Times* and wanted to duplicate it in her high school geometry class, so her questions were different from Odessa's, but just as important to her. Alan seemed bound to find out why this class was so successful. He was very positive with each of the kids I saw him interact with, and he looked like he believed strongly in what the class was doing.

Then there was Jim, a teacher with twenty years of experience in the mathematics classroom. He stood on the fringes for nearly half the class time. He sort of circled the class, like a vulture looking for a meal. Jim was the one who caused the most discomfort for me, observing from afar and writing things down in a notebook.

At one point he was near the door just as Arcy came in from the group outside. I didn't hear what she said, but in no time she had Jim outside with her group. I couldn't help but wonder what was going on out there. The group consisted of Arcy—Chris's best friend, Carmen—the spokesperson for Larry's Metric Circle, Patty—the girl with the lines that "ducked" under one another, and Sergio—the football player.

I didn't have time to go outside because the reflection group wanted me to observe what they had found. After that, I was heading for the door to check on the outside group when Bernie, who had been failing the class badly, caught me and convinced me to come look over the basketball presentation he had planned for tomorrow.

I was about to sit down in Bernie's place, next to Larry and Alicia, when Bernie asked for a volunteer from the audience. The rest of the group raised my hand for me and voilà, I was the volunteer. The first thing he had me do was hold the basketball in such a way that the great circle around the ball was vertical to the ground. Bernie then took two pieces of masking tape, each about two feet in length, and placed them both tangent to the sphere perpendicular to the great circle. This meant that the two pieces of tape were horizontal to the ground, parallel with each other, and one end of each piece of tape was stuck on the ball.

I could tell from the tone in Bernie's voice that he was about to perform magic as he asked, "Are these two pieces of masking tape parallel?" in a nothing-up-my-sleeve tone of voice.

I had nodded my agreement, and Bernie took each piece of tape and flattened it down on the basketball. He turned the basketball over and the two pieces of tape met on the other side. It is true that two lines that are parallel on a plane are not necessarily parallel on a sphere. So I tested Bernie with the argument that there could be two pieces of tape on the basketball that were parallel. I took two pieces of tape and wrapped them both horizontally around the ball.

Then Larry spoke up as if he were directing this demonstration, "Go ahead, Bernie, show him."

Bernie looked down confidently at these two supposedly parallel lines and said, "See the way the outsides of the tape are crinkled up? That means that they don't want to bend that way." He returned the pieces of tape to the original, smooth, intersecting positions.

My first reaction was to argue that inanimate things such as lines don't have have the capability of "wanting" or "not wanting" to bend. But what Bernie said next eliminated my reaction altogether.

"My friend was watching a show on public television, and the guy on it said that the universe is curved. If that's true, then all parallel lines must meet."

Wow, what a proof. I used to spend hours and hours trying to help the students in my traditional geometry classes understand how to take information from a variety of sources and pull it together for a proof. And here this guy, who is failing the class, comes up with a unique, creative, and internally logical proof.

I was speechless, which pleased Larry and the group no end. I'm glad there was no photographer to immortalize that moment as had been done in the *L.A. Times.*

Bernie's demonstration was great for all of us, and I couldn't wait for him to present it to the class tomorrow. I just wish I could have had him demonstrate it for all the visitors, not just the three who happened to be in the group at that time.

Before I had time to consider my options, the bell rang and I had to get the investigation sheets gathered in and all the materials returned to the right places. The group working on the computer had a hard time getting finished and as a result stayed around until the tardy bell rang for sixth period. Many of the kids don't have a class after No Book, but those who do need passes to their next class if they are late. This meant I had to write excuses for the two computer people who had another class.

Group Seven decided that the concept of earthquake-proof, interlocking bricks was not to be passed over. In areas that are very earthquake-prone the idea would be helpful. They decided the best idea would be to place the building on rubber shocks. I listened politely while the visiting teachers and Toby waited, then I suggested that they present the idea after Bernie's presentation tomorrow.

No Book has space in it for the discussion of real-life topics such as earthquake preparations. I wonder if anything will ever come of the earthquake-proof bricks or the rubber shocks? My job at that point was to write more passes to class for this group. I can't help wondering about all the late passes this class causes me to write, but I guess if it were a problem I'd get some feedback from their teachers.

I was just sitting down when my department head, Yvette, entered with soft drinks and snacks for the visiting teachers. Before I got a soft drink, in came Jim and the group from outside. They had been laying out a circle on the blacktop with a diameter of 100 feet. Then they were checking to see if the circle curved or if there actually were short straight sides. And then they were looking at arcs and possible angles. As they entered it appeared that Jim had become one of the group. All five were animatedly talking about their work outside. The kids were so enthusiastic about the assistance they had received from Jim that they asked if he could be a guest speaker in the class someday. I hadn't thought about guest speakers from outside the school, but I guess it couldn't hurt.

Only one of the people in their group needed a pass, so they were quickly on their way. After this final interruption we sat down to talk—the eight visiting teachers, Toby, Yvette, and myself.

I opened the door by asking if there were any questions. That was all there was in the way of introduction. The group spent the whole time asking questions of me and of each other until way past the hour that was allotted—not too different from a No Book class.

The discussion began with a pointed question from Barbara: "I really enjoyed this, but things don't function like this every day, do they? What did you set up especially for this visit?"

I told her my thought process and how I had wished that it could have been planned. I explained that today was not an aberration, but a typical example of the way things are in the No Book class. Some days are better and some worse. (I felt like telling her she should have been here yesterday, but decided against it.) From here, the discussion erupted.

Harold said he had entered the class today expecting to see some fake classroom. He said his expectations of the No Book class weren't very high. He is in his second year of teaching, and I think he wants to help students succeed in math, but he believes that some people can do math and others can't. At least that was what he thought prior to today. His last statement during our discussion was the best. He felt he had to take a few days to consider this experience, but that maybe his can/can't image of mathematics is in error.

Odessa has been teaching for a long time. She said she had come here in hopes of finding some mathematics to take to the calculus classes she teaches at her prep school. "I read about the new proof to the Pythagorean Theorem in the *Los Angeles Times* and I wanted to know if there were any other mathematical discoveries taking place in this class," she said. She went on to say that there was plenty of mathematics discovery taking place, but not the way she had planned. Instead of learning new mathematics, she had experienced the excitement the students found in their discoveries. She said she was going to see how she could fit this No Book kind of discovery into calculus, even if it wasn't all "real" calculus that her students discovered.

Ted asked how much instruction I had given the students on the *Supposer.* He was impressed by their knowledge of the computer. That was one of those questions I had dreaded. I had to admit that my knowledge of the *Supposer* was practically nil, except for some time I spent with the software at MSTI last summer. I told Ted that the kids had a much better understanding of how the *Supposer* operated than I did. It was extremely uncomfortable to admit that sort of weakness in a group like this, but no one seemed to react judgmentally.

Espy and Alan were colleagues at the same school and were interested in trying a No Book class. Espy asked the entire group for their opinions as to the feasibility of duplicating No Book geometry on other campuses. The responses were mixed. It seems the visitors were still not sure whether this was a set-up.

At opposite ends of the attitude scale were Jim and Susan. Jim admitted he came to this "site visit," as he called it, to discredit the No Book concept. Susan came from a school in Long Beach and was so positive about this class before she walked in that it probably could have been a disaster and still received a rave review from her. She was so certain that giving responsibility and freedom to high school people was the key to their growth and learning. Her visit here had to reinforce her beliefs; I'm glad it worked out so well. It's amazing how the attitudes of outside people affect how I think about this class.

I was feeling really good at this point, and then Jim got his notebook out. In it he had evaluated the first half of the class. He read off his notes to all of us.

Pre-class note: We arrived during the final minutes of the previous period to find the teacher standing on a desk in the middle of the classroom, supposedly teaching the class. What reason can there be for such unsafe behavior?

1. The homework was collected at the door by a student, not the teacher of the class.
2. The homework was given to a group of students before the teacher had a chance to grade or even check it.
3. A student got a basketball out of the closet and threw it across the room to another student.
4. The teacher left the room to get something, leaving the students alone and unsupervised.
5. Additional note: The PLUS project director, instead of supervising the experience of the teachers, was involved with the students and oblivious to the needs of the visiting teachers.
6. Students were defacing school property by vandalizing the mirror—with the full support of the teacher.
7. A group of four students were allowed to leave the classroom unsupervised.

8. One group was allowed, even encouraged, to discuss the negative fourth dimension—a fictional topic with no connection with the curriculum of high school geometry.

9. One of the outside students interrupted the class and wanted some help outside. I volunteered. This gave me the opportunity to see what was going on unsupervised.

With this he closed his notebook and began to just talk.

"I came here with the idea of discrediting this No Book concept. I believe very strongly that high school students need a text. I know that the texts are not perfect and need supplemental material, but a text is necessary for the basic curriculum and order. It bothered me that by not using a textbook this class was getting such publicity. So I took it upon myself to examine this class and expose the sham. That's why the notebook and the notes. But the most important part of my examination took place after I stopped taking notes. What happened outside without the teacher is the real story of this class.

"I was taken outside by this young lady named Arcy and treated with great respect. The students had run into a problem creating a circle with a diameter of one hundred feet, and they were looking for advice. I gave them my advice and helped them draw the circle they wanted. We couldn't draw it at first because we needed such a long string for the radius. They solved this problem by going to the shop class to get a long enough piece of string. While we were drawing the circle they asked questions. How did I know it would be a perfect circle? What about stones on the blacktop? What constitutes a straight line? How do we know that pi is correct? Why are circle degrees measured from the center of a circle?

"Then it struck me. The students in this class really wanted to know the answers. Some of their questions were simple and others so complex that I had difficulty answering them, but the students had a vested interest in each of the questions, so they were interested in each of the answers.

"Something else I observed was that the students not only treated me with respect, they respected each other. They listened to the person who was talking whether it was one of them or me. I may have gotten more respect here than back in my own classroom.

"When the bell rang, Sergio had one more thing he wanted to investigate and so we spent a few minutes working on it. As I watched Sergio, I couldn't help thinking that if he were in my class he'd be sitting in the back, failing the class and causing problems. But not here. Even on the way back into class he was asking me things as if they really mattered to him.

"If I didn't know any better I would have thought I was set up. While I was out there a student who said she was failing the class asked me if I would be able to come back in a week and see what else they had discovered. This interest from a person failing the class?

"Another student in that group asked me if I could come back and speak to the rest of the class as a guest speaker. She didn't impress me as a student that would be interested in geometry, but here she was seeking further information from a stranger.

"The comments I read to you from my notebook a few minutes ago are still valid. Some things that go on in this class do need to be reevaluated. But the biggest reevaluation may be of the way high school mathematics is taught."

What an assessment of the class, and what a change! Jim made a number of good points that I need to consider—especially the defacing of school property and the lack of supervision. There are so many things taking place in this class that are hard to evaluate, but this is a learning experience for me, too.

I doubt that this little experiment is going to begin a revolution in the teaching of mathematics, but after the change it made in that teacher, who knows what the actual value of this class is? With Bernie's basketball view of the universe and "wanting" lines, the negative fourth dimension reversing time travel, the homework collection and class definitions, the mirror reflections, straight-sided circles, and earthquake-proof buildings, I guess our visitors saw what they came for. I'm glad things worked out so well.

February 23

Bernie made his presentation today and the class seemed to enjoy it. They understood him the first time better than I had. Maybe it was because they weren't encumbered by the need to place his discovery into some category like spherical geometry. Alicia questioned making parallel lines go around the ball, and Bernie responded with his argument about lines "not wanting to bend and crinkle up." I could tell it didn't sit well with Alicia, but she reserved comment.

When Bernie came up with the Stephen Hawking quote about the universe being curved, it didn't quiet the class as it had me. They kept questioning it. In fact, Bernie got kind of lost as all the groups began discussing, arguing, and in the end disagreeing with the idea of a curved universe. Having reached this conclusion, the class voted not to include Bernie's presentation in the book. He wasn't as affected as I would have thought, but one person in his group was.

In the couple of minutes remaining in the class Larry did a very Carmen-like thing: he sought a compromise. He asked the class if Bernie's idea should be put in the back of the book, like an appendix. He said, "If this curved universe thing ever proved to be true, we want people in the future to know what our class has discovered and then they can build on it from there." There wasn't even any discussion. The vote was unanimous.

Chapter 18

Chris Returns
(Chris's thoughts—February 26)

"Y ou return home now or you're out of this family forever and never welcome here again!" My dad thought the most powerful threat he could make. But it's only a good threat if the person being threatened considers "home" a place they want to go to.

After I had lived a month in Mexico with my grandparents, my father issued that ultimatum and I was positive it was out of desperation. To him it may have sounded like a terrible threat, but I didn't receive it that way. Six months ago I would have, but I think I've changed a lot from that girl. My father has used his ultimate threat, and now he knows that there is no next step for him. Who's in control of my life now? The only control he has—or anyone has—is the amount of control I choose to give them. That was always true, only I never knew it, till now.

The fact is, I decided a week before the "threat" that I was coming back to El Monte to finish school. I have just three semesters to go (if they let my first semester grades count). I knew there were things there that I wanted to finish and people I wanted to see. Letty knew all about my decision and she knows that the reason I returned was my own choice, but my dad doesn't, and I think I like it better that way.

Mexico was okay and my grandparents were really good to me, as they always have been ever since I was small. Either they like me especially or they treat all family special. Even after I arrived as a "runaway" (I always thought of myself more as a "walkaway," because I did it so calmly) and they were put in an uncomfortable position, they never showed that they were less than really truly happy to see me. While I was at their house, they acted as if I was there on a vacation. I slept in, and I just relaxed a lot. Of course, I helped around the house. And they needed that, because my grandfather isn't as strong and healthy as he used to be. It's not that he's sick, he's just sort of wearing down with age. He can still do everything, it's just slower and he rests more frequently than before. He used to work in his garden every day. In his free time, he used to fish and work on cars. I didn't know anyone who was as active as he was.

I remember once when I was a little girl, he and I walked all over the town of Guadalajara and then hiked up the big hill behind their house. My grandfather carried me on his back all the way up and he wasn't even breathing hard. That's the way I'll always think of him, no matter how old he gets. He'll always be a strong man to me.

When I was down there doing a lot of nothing, I had a chance to think about my life and about what I want out of my future. David would have been proud of me, and maybe he will be when I see him this summer. I'm going to do that, not to try to win him back, but to let him know he was very special in my life and that I'm doing okay now. I decided to make something of myself and to not be so influenced by my family or other people. I don't mean I'm going to ignore what people say to me, actually I plan to listen more carefully now. I'll listen to what they say and then I'll decide if it's right for me. I think everyone needs help to become who they want to be. The free time to think about things that I had in Mexico made this clearer for me.

I came back here to make a new start in my life and I think I can do it. I know that I'm here because I want to be. I know that my father still thinks he has control over me and it doesn't bother me. And I know where I'm going now and that makes everything better than it ever has been. I just hope I don't have to run away every time I need to look at things. How did David ever manage to keep things straight in his head and know where he was going no matter what? Maybe once you make a decision you don't need to go to Mexico to reevaluate. I sure hope not.

The first thing I did when I got back to El Monte, even before I went to my house, was go to Mr. Healy's class to see him. In the letter he wrote to me while I was in Mexico, he said there would always be a place for me in his geometry class and that he hoped I'd be back. He might have just written that to make me feel good, but I don't think he was just saying it. I think he really felt that way. In his letter he said that I am an important person. He also said that I made him feel good when I wrote in my note to him about miracles happening in the geometry class. I could hardly remember what I wrote. It seems strange that Mr. Healy would be so affected by my note. Maybe I can write well enough to change things. I've always wanted to write, but I was afraid to really try, except in my diary and on assignments. Maybe that's something I can think more about when I get to college.

Yes, college! That's what I decided when I was in Mexico. I've always wanted to be a sixth-grade teacher, but I never thought I had a chance. While I was in Mexico I decided that I not only have a chance, I am the one who can make it happen, and no one else. It'll be hard, but it can't happen if I don't try. To get there, I knew I had to set minigoals, and the first one is to finish high school.

When I went to see Mr. Healy I wasn't sure how he'd react. I interrupted one of his classes and he smiled a "welcome back" smile at me, but just went on teaching algebra. So even after I got there I wasn't sure what he was going to say, or how he was going to react to me. Then he gave an assignment, so there was a break in the class, and he came over and gave me the biggest hug. I was back, there was a place for me, and now I was sure I could do it.

I stayed in his class the rest of the day, even during lunchtime, and we talked about everything. He says he supports me in anything I say or do. It's like no matter what I decide he knows it'll be right for me. But even if it wasn't, he'd always be there to help me if I really needed it. That's how I like things to be now—on my own, but feeling support from others.

When fifth period came around I was a little nervous because I didn't know what to expect from the other people in the class. I guess the only reaction I didn't expect was just plain acceptance, which is what I got. When they came in, I could tell they were glad to see me, but within a few minutes the group I was in wasn't talking about my being gone. They were talking about something called "invisible" geometry. It was like I never left and the two months were invisible. Personally, I don't think invisible geometry exists. (How could you know if it did, you couldn't see it anyway?)

That afternoon when I got home, I knew the time I spent away wasn't invisible to my parents. They treated me very differently, almost like I was a stranger. Everything seemed to be different. It was kind of like when my father changed when he stopped drinking. No one came out and said anything, but you could tell something was different and would never be like it was before. Now all the problems couldn't be blamed on alcohol. When my father wasn't dependent on alcohol anymore, the family tried to ignore the problems and hoped they would go away. I've changed, too. I'm no longer dependent either on anything, but myself. Maybe my parents will ignore the changes and hope they go away.

At least there haven't been any blowups so far. But I know it'll happen in the future. So I'm just going to try to be prepared and ready to avoid conflict when it's not necessary and to face it when it is. I'm not going to pretend it isn't there. When something is wrong, you can't ignore it. It won't work itself out and go away. If you think that, you're just fooling yourself.

Letty and my brothers haven't changed, except Letty and I are closer now than we've ever been. I think when you share something as secret and personal as we did, you just naturally get closer. Letty was my only contact with home for so many weeks, and she was under lots of pressure from our parents and school people. One of the most important things in my mind is being able to trust a person, and I sure know I can trust Letty. She always wanted to be like me, but it wasn't until now that I was sure I could trust her.

Letty and I used to have this thing that we did, but now it's been updated. It used to be, I'd say, "I'll be the first one in our family to graduate from high school."

She'd say, "...and I'll be the second."

So when I told my whole family I was going to college and become a teacher, she said, "...and I'll be the second teacher."

My parents weren't nearly as supportive of the idea as I thought they'd be, but they didn't say much because the communication in my family is so limited right now. At least they weren't negative, so maybe I chose the best time to tell them. They operate under some pretty strange rules and right now the rules seem to be that they can't react strongly.

Talking about a strong reaction, though—Mr. Healy was so excited about my teacher decision that he went straight to his desk and got his college book out. We discussed colleges for me to think about. We talked about what I had to do to get into each, how much they cost, what financial aid was available, and when I needed to apply. He didn't waste any time. I don't know which school I'll go to yet, but there's plenty of time for that.

I wonder which schools have good football programs and also have good medical schools attached. Wait a minute, first I've got to go and find out about what's going to happen with my first semester grades and plan from there … but it wouldn't hurt to check into schools that offer teaching, medicine, and football (and are probably near the beach as well).

Chapter 19

ط.

Facilitating, Not Teaching
(Chip's thoughts—March 6)

T hings have happened so fast since the end of the first semester that I've hardly had time to think. There hasn't even been time to figure out how things are going, but spring vacation will be here in a few weeks. Maybe I can get some perspective then, and I can use the break.

At the start of the No Book class, I may have been thought of as the fountain of knowledge, but now I'm just another shmuck (that's Larry's word) with an opinion. In the eyes of the students, my opinion is worthy of consideration but bears no exceptional weight by virtue of my position. Is this a positive or a negative about the class? This is something to be considered when there's more time to evaluate. I was never more aware of the loss of my authority than when the *Times* article came out with that picture. I'm sure no one else remembers, but of the dozens of pictures that guy took, that photograph in particular shows my loss of the normal teacher status.

So now I really have changed from the role of teacher in the class to that of facilitator. Anyway, I still give the tests, analyze the information turned in, and take attendance—though this last is hardly necessary because no one is ever absent except for Christina (make that Chris), and she returned the other day to my class after being in Mexico for six weeks.

The girl that returned was a much more self-confident, directed person than the one I remember from before Christmas. Her situation at home wasn't good, from what I understand, but usually running away complicates things rather than simplifies them. However, Chris ran away in a most responsible way. She kept in touch with people like her sister, the school, and myself. Furthermore, she went to her cousin's and then to another relative's home. I don't know a whole lot about the process of running away, and I suspect it varies with every individual, but I would guess that it isn't frequently handled with this amount of control.

When Chris returned to El Monte, she came straight to school to see me. That surely made me feel special. She's looking more toward her future now, and I helped her find some of the specifics for that future. I still don't know what happened to her in those two months away, but in her case it seems to have helped her get things sorted out.

When she needed help after running away, she obviously found people willing to help and take her in. My daughters and I returned the pigeon we took in (and named after Chris) to its home in the wild. Both the pigeon and the girl found safe places to stay when they needed it. Both are now healed and ready to flourish in their chosen places. After my daughters' tearful good-byes to their pigeon Chris, we went out to breakfast, where we learned that the *L.A. Times* article was in that day's paper.

Since that day, the interest in the No Book class has increased even more. For some reason the *Times* article ended up in the Metro section rather than the San Gabriel section. That meant that regardless of location, anyone buying a copy of the *Times* got the article. As a result, I've received letters, phone calls, and inquiries from all over, including San Francisco, Boston, Salton Sea, Carpenteria, and a special letter from Long Beach. It read:

Dear Mr. Healy,

I'm writing this letter in response to the article that appeared in the Feb. 12 edition of the *L.A. Times.*

While I'm sure the eagerness of and results of the students you teach is reward enough, I'd like to express my gratitude that teachers such as yourself, who realize the importance of thinking as opposed to rote memorization, are recognized and given the freedom to teach as they see fit.

When I was in high school I was an eager, inquisitive, yet frustrated student. I attended a school which catered to the average student and my mind was rarely challenged. I found no place for original thinking. Like many other students, I lost interest in high school. I appreciated the quote from the article: "Healy said his major role is to bounce the students' ideas back to them, without telling them whether they are right or wrong." I would have flourished under a teacher like yourself as I am sure your students do.

I feel that you are providing a wonderful service by equipping your students with the desire and ability to think in addition to confidence in their own thought processes so that they can be above average in life.

The class is special in the eyes of people from all over. People visit the classroom almost every day from all sorts of places—high school teachers, college professors, authors. The unusual thing about it is that no matter who is visiting, the kids are not impressed. It doesn't even affect them. They have their own tasks to accomplish, and no matter what the interruption, they aren't distracted.

I've told the class repeatedly how unique they are, but it has no effect. Why is that? After all the publicity and all the visitors, I'd think that the students would begin to get an idea that they were accomplishing something at least a little unusual. If they are aware of the stir they are causing, they certainly don't show it.

The week before vacation I'm planning to give them the SATGEOM test, which I made up from the sample tests in the back of one of those SAT study guides. I took a total of 40 geometry questions from the book, and I'm going to test all the geometry classes on this information before the vacation. We'll see how the No Book class compares to the other classes at this point.

I know how much I want the class to do well and make up for that five percent difference at the semester, but Toby (from PLUS) made that difference seem less significant. She said that according to the California Math Framework the class is moving in the right direction, even if their mathematical knowledge is presently less than they may have gained with a more traditional approach. According to the framework, which will be affecting schools in the next few years, the No Book class is right on target because the kids are: (1) communicating mathematically, (2) working together, (3) problem solving, and (4) creating mathematics.

As I look at the No Book students today and compare them with who they were last September, I see major differences. They not only communicate better, but they listen to each other and consider the opinions of everyone. They have learned to stand up for what they believe in and, when it's necessary, to compromise to reach an agreement. They have taken the responsibility of learning and understanding seriously, and they know it is up to them whether or not they succeed. I think they truly care about each other. It's kind of like a family in that there are disagreements and disharmony within the class (even within the groups at times), but they stick together when challenged from outside.

Most important, they are learning to rely on themselves. Their self-esteem, collectively and individually, has vastly improved since September. I believe this carries over to their lives outside the classroom as well, but I have no proof of that. That's one of the obvious weaknesses of assessing this class. The progress they make as individuals can't be measured.

This class has caught the imagination of so many people that I've been asked to speak to a group of a hundred or so teachers at the NCTM (National Council of Teachers of Mathematics) convention in Chicago after spring break.

I'll have spring vacation to prepare and that should be enough time. I need to get away from all the publicity and activities related to this class for a while. During the vacation I'm going to use the *Supposer* to prove beyond a doubt that Edmund's proof works. Now, if I can only make it to vacation!

Larry's thoughts—March 22

The first progress reports of the second semester just arrived and I did all right, considering I'm a senior and seniors are supposed to kick back the last semester. In fact, except for the C in geometry class, I had a 3.0 average. Shit, man, that's the best I've done since my sophomore year. It could have been the best ever, if I hadn't made the decision to stay in that geometry class for the rest of the year.

I stayed for two reasons: First, our class did nearly as well as the book classes on that final so we're not as far behind as I figured. Second, that class couldn't survive without me so I took pity on them. I know it's not exactly logical for me to take pity on them, when it's my last semester. Heck, if I don't do it, who will?

So I'm still in there and I've got them all doing okay. Even the grades are improving. And they're listening to me better than ever. They may be agreeing with me less now, but there's no more fiascoes like our Metric Circle, where Carmen had to rescue me. Not only are they listening better, they're getting smarter, so what they're saying makes more sense.

Still, as good as we're getting, sometimes Enoch, Shawn, Gerardo, or I have a bad day. It just happens to seniors. When it does, Healy sends the person outside to cool off. It doesn't bother me, I just kick back and relax. But after listening to Gerardo today, I think he takes it a little more personally.

Let me set the scene. The class just left and the room is empty except for Healy, Shawn, Enoch, Gerardo, and me. Gerardo is sort of stalking Healy, who's looking at the papers that the groups turned in. When he looks up, before he knows it Gerardo attacks, "I do one little thing in this class and 'Boom,' you kick me out of the room!"

I sit back ready to watch a conflict of world-class proportion. I love conflicts, that's why I know I could be a great lawyer if I wanted to. I'm waiting to hear from the defense and what do you think Healy's doing? He looks like he's an actor on stage.

He's not preparing a defense, he's rehearsing, "Boom! No. Boooom. Nope. Baoom! No, that's not right. How did you say it?"

Gerry's totally amazed by this turn of events. He doesn't know how to respond, so he retreats into sarcasm. "Did I stutter?" he asks.

"Nope, I just want to get my 'Boom' exactly like yours. Let's be realistic, it's the spring semester and seniors think they should be able to kick back. I understand that, but the four of you are leaders in the class, and when one of you chooses to take the day off, it affects the whole class. From now on when I see one of you needs some kick-back time, I'll just say 'Boom.' It won't have to be loud and it won't affect the rest of the class. You're the leaders and you don't want to disturb the class. When you get a 'Boom,' just go outside and relax until I get out there and we can talk."

Shit, we didn't even argue. The way Gerardo had stalked and attacked him, I expected Healy to be on the defensive. Instead, he says we're the class leaders, he understands about seniors, and he knows we want what's best for the class. Who's going to argue with that? So, ever since that day if any one of us is having an off day, Healy just looks at the person and mouths "boom." Whoever it is goes outside and kicks back for a few minutes. What the hell—it makes things easier on him and the class and it lets us out whenever we really need it.

It hasn't happened very often to any of us, because what's going on in that class is really getting interesting with all the visitors and outside attention. All this attention is a good experience for me because it's something I have to get used to for the future. For the others, this will probably be their only experience with fame.

I don't think they know how to handle it. Here it is, their moment in the spotlight, and they're reacting like it's no big deal. I've been in this class long enough to know what's going on. Healy's smart, but he's no miracle worker. All these teachers, professors, and writers don't seem to understand that, so we're getting all the glory. I can handle it, but I think we ought to be getting paid for our time.

All I'm saying is, if they're taking our time, we should be compensated. We've got to go for the bucks now, while the class is still big news. The chance for compensation will be over when we get back from spring vacation. It's a good thing spring vacation is nearly here, I need a break. That's the one thing I'd miss if I didn't go to college... the vacations.

Chapter 20

&

Oh, I Know
(Chip's thoughts—April 10)

Before I left school the day before spring vacation, I finished tabulating the results from the SATGEOM tests from all four geometry classes. The results were still not what I'd hoped for, but at least I knew this exam was testing the SAT knowledge they would need. The average score in my No Book class remained five percent below the combined averages of the other classes. It's not that big a difference and it could have been worse, but I was disappointed.

On the first day of spring vacation, I sat down with my Apple IIe and the *Supposer* in the relative quiet of my study and set about verifying the Park Proof. The *Supposer* isn't perfect. It is a remarkably useful tool for a traditional geometry class that studies traditional things, but it doesn't always do what the students in the No Book class want. I've been aware of that shortcoming, but it was just another obstacle and those kids have become experts in overcoming obstacles. It caused such frustration for Gerardo in the beginning that he gave up on it, but the others have profited by this unique software.

I'm no expert with the *Supposer*, and I kept thinking about my lack of expertise as I manipulated the on-screen information to try to duplicate on a random right triangle the picture Edmund had presented. It wasn't easy to duplicate because the *Supposer* was definitely not made with the Park Proof in mind. However, the *Supposer* does all the measuring. I knew if I could get the construction right, it would verify the proof. It took quite a while, and I made a number of mistakes before I finally arrived at the picture I thought represented what Edmund had demonstrated.

When I hit the final key for verification, I received results from the picture I had constructed that did not agree with Edmund. Unfortunately, I had no time to check my results. I knew I could duplicate the picture later, so I discounted the results and planned to try again later in the vacation.

Things got busy and I didn't get back to the computer and *Supposer* until the last day of vacation. I carefully inputted the information and the picture appeared on the screen.

One of the things I like best about the *Supposer* is that after doing the construction with the computer you just press a button and the results appear on the screen to verify your conjecture. With everything done, I pushed that final key and waited for verification. It didn't happen. Again the figures didn't confirm Edmund's proof.

I still figured it must have been my mistake. I repeated the process, having my wife watch every step to check my work. She knew all about Edmund's proof and looked forward to being a part of the verification. She agreed that I made no error, but the results on the screen didn't verify Edmund's proof. In fact, they proved he was incorrect. The Park Proof had been sent out to high school teachers, college professors, and mathematicians across the country and evidently no one had ever checked its credibility.

The following day at the beginning of fifth period, I stationed myself on the opposite side of the class from the group that Edmund was in. Then I announced that the Park Proof was flawed. I told Edmund I was sorry, but the *Supposer* had proven it. The class was extremely disappointed, but Edmund seemed to take it in stride and wasn't nearly as upset as his classmates.

Later in the class, after the groups began to function smoothly, I went over to talk to Edmund about his proof.

"Edmund, maybe I shouldn't have told everyone at the same time, but I couldn't think of a good way to announce it. I'm really sorry, but your proof just doesn't work."

He just looked up at me and very matter-of-factly said, "Oh, I know. It only works if the ratio of the legs is two to one. But that's the kind of right triangle that most people draw anyway, isn't it?"

I was dumbfounded. This high school freshman had taken us all in and no one had discovered his secret. We had sent out dozens of manipulatives demonstrating his proof and the only one that was questioned turned out to have been drawn incorrectly.

Thinking he must have discovered this discrepancy at some point and not been able to share it due to the publicity his proof had received, I asked, "How long have you known about this?"

"Since the day before I presented it to the class, but I didn't want to confuse anyone."

He does think on another level from the rest of us!

The remainder of that week the groups worked on either three-dimensional stuff or the now-flawed Park Proof. They found that it was definitely close; perhaps with a little help there might be a legitimate Park Proof someday. Regardless of the flaw, I planned to present the Park Proof at the NCTM conference in Chicago and at least offer it as an alternative way to teach the Pythagorean Theorem.

Chicago was a lot more fun than I had expected. I only attended a few sessions at the conference, but I saw a White Sox game and a Georgia O'Keefe art exhibit, visited much of the city, and met a lot of people. Richard, a good friend whom I knew through PLUS and MSTI, and Yvette were my partners in sightseeing and missing much of the conference.

Richard was a math teacher in Inglewood. One evening we were sitting in the lounge on the top floor of the Sears Building. After talking about the No Book class and the *L.A. Times* article, he asked me if I was ready for tomorrow's speech.

I hesitated, having tried to postpone the thought of my "payment" for the trip. "Yeah...I guess."

Richard's response to my moment of hesitation was really helpful. (He's like that though, always using just the right words to plant a thought in a listener's mind.) All he said was, "You'll do great, I know it. Just be yourself up there. You are going to be yourself, right?"

I responded as if it were a silly question, but I knew that what was written on my computer paper in the suitcase wasn't me. I also knew that Richard was right. They had brought me to Chicago to speak, so they should hear me, not something else. The first thing I did the next day was to throw out the suitcase speech. Then I found a stationery store and bought some supplies.

When I talk to adults, which seems to happen more and more these days, I feel better with visual aids. So I made posters for a picture of the Park Proof, information about Alicia's PLIT and Larry's Metric Circle, and an overview of how the class functioned.

Then I went to see Grace, my computer friend from EDC, who was in charge of organizing the session. I asked her if the session called for formal attire or if dress was casual. Nikes and jeans were fine with her, so I was set. I was going to be me.

Suffice it to say, the talk went extremely well. Almost every one of the nearly one hundred math teachers listened to every word of each story. They were genuinely interested in the class. In fact, when I mentioned the five percent difference in the SATGEOM scores they immediately deluged me with excuses. They assured me that regardless of the five percent, which they thought was insignificant to begin with, the No Book kids would retain what they'd learned longer and do better on the SAT next fall. One thing is for sure: people want to believe in this class.

After my speech there was a question-and-answer time. A teacher from Philadelphia asked, "What does your administration say? My administration would never let me try anything new."

Before I had a chance to respond, I felt a hand on my shoulder and Yvette whispered firmly to me, "Let me handle this one." One of her buttons had been pressed. Yvette blasted right in: "Don't give me this crap about administration. That's only an excuse teachers hide behind. If you want to do something, go for it. I am sick and tired of teachers saying, 'I can't do anything because of the administration.' They have no idea what goes on in your classroom behind closed doors. You're there for the students, not the administration. If you can help students learn in a way that the administration might not agree with, then do it. It's your job to teach students, not to make excuses."

I was concerned that the lady who asked the question might shrink into oblivion, but as Yvette spoke the teachers listened. I think her response made people really think.

One of the other panelists suggested, "I've always found it easier to try a new approach before consulting the administration. They try to block so many innovations. I find it's much easier to apologize after the fact, than it is to get prior approval."

I came away from the speech with a new set of questions. Why are people so enthusiastic about this class? I'm not knocking the success, but how can people who don't know me or the class make excuses for the test scores? Why did no one find the flaw in the Park Proof? Why are so many people visiting the class?

The answers aren't clear, but I am convinced they have to do with people wanting to believe that there is a solution out there someplace—one that doesn't take a superhero to implement. The need for solutions to the problems with young people is so evident in our society right now. There are a few teaching superheroes, like Jaime Escalante, but the search continues for answers for the regular teacher.

I am one of those regular teachers. I know what kind of a person I was a year ago in the classroom, and I know I haven't changed all that much. If what I'm doing with the No Book class is so special, then I think the answer lies inside a majority of teachers. Teachers are creative and can do a great deal if given time. People think that increasing the number of hours in the classroom will increase the amount of education accordingly. I don't disagree with the logic in that idea, but I know that we, as teachers, waste incredible amounts of classroom time now. Instead of increasing the days or hours, which only works if the kids are willing to concentrate for the increased time, why not reduce the days and require as a part of the teaching calendar each year a MSTI-type experience for the teachers?

I don't believe every teacher can teach in the shoes of a Jaime Escalante (I know I couldn't), and I don't believe every teacher should attempt a No Book class, but I do believe that almost every teacher has the capability to develop an effective style of relating to students and helping them learn. I believe each teacher wants to improve. It's going to involve some risk taking, but I believe all teachers are capable of creating unique miracles of their own.

Chapter 21

ટ▲.

The Chris Shape
(Chris's thoughts—April 22)

How many people have a shape named after them? I discovered a three-dimensional shape called the Chris Shape. The original idea for the Chris Shape came from one of the letters that we got about our article in the *Times*. I took what the person was describing and tried to draw a picture on the board of what I thought it looked like. It's hard to draw three-dimensional things on a two-dimensional chalkboard. Mr. Healy said he had a difficult time understanding anything in three dimensions. The only way he could do it was to have an example of the object he could hold in his hands. Either he's not too bright or he's rather sneaky because I spent the whole weekend building what I thought the letter was talking about.

I used those big index cards to build my shape. First, I constructed three congruent isosceles right triangles. Next I put all the right angles together and glued the matching sides together. Then I measured the hypotenuse and cut out an equilateral triangle whose sides were the same length as the hypotenuse. Last, I glued the sides of the equilateral triangle to the hypotenuses.

The Chris Shape construction isn't as exciting as the Park Proof, but it's mine. I still think the Park Proof is valid, no matter what anyone says, because it's the first time I ever understood the Pythagorean Theorem.

It took me a long time to figure out how to build the Chris Shape and I made a lot of mistakes before I got it right. Six months ago I could never have spent as much time working on the construction at home as I did this weekend. My parents would have found something else for me to do. But ever since I came back from Mexico, they are kind of subdued. They still have their opinions and they still like to yell, but it's different than it used to be.

Before I ran away their arguments sounded like, "Chris, do this … or else," and I never wanted to find out what the "or else" was. Now their arguments sound like they are saying, "Chris, do this … please don't disagree." It seems like they are using the same words, but the tone or something has changed. Maybe they were always afraid that I might disagree, but I never heard it in their voices, or maybe it was never there because they never considered that I might really disobey them. Or maybe it's just the same as it always was, only now I don't feel so helpless because I know there are other options. Whatever the reason, it made it possible for me to work almost the entire weekend without interruption.

It was a lot of hard work, but I eventually built a total of four congruent (I think that word works in three-dimensional shapes) Chris Shapes using the big index cards. I brought them to Mr. Healy and we had a long discussion after class. He convinced me that I hadn't built what the letter said at all. That's when he called it a Chris Shape. I liked that, because it became part of the vocabulary for the class.

Since then there's been investigations into the Chris Shape, especially the volume. One group went to the science department to get materials like fine sand and beakers and scales to measure volume. Our group thought we could build a cube out of Chris shapes if we could only find out how many Chris Shapes there are in a cube. It took some doing because four of them make a shell of the cube with a big empty section in the middle. We found out you could fill that space with a triangular pyramid made out of equilateral triangles. After some more work we discovered that the volume of a Chris Shape is one sixth the volume of the cube. Discovering new information is fun, especially if it is named after you.

While I was away Mr. Healy assigned projects for the second semester. I was hoping that maybe he wouldn't make me do one. The other day he told me that the project is optional, but that it would really help my grade. I need to get good grades because the colleges will be looking at my grades soon. I didn't want to do the project, but it's not so difficult now to think about that kind of stuff because I know where I'm headed. I know that the project would be good for me and for my future. And I know that I can do a project on something I'm really interested in.

Like everything else that happens in that class, there are no rules on the project, except that it has to have something to do with mathematics. Seeing as I'm going to be teaching sixth grade, I thought my project would have to do with math in the lower grades.

I think mathematics is taught in the wrong order from the time you are in kindergarten. For instance, I think decimals and integers should be taught with the rest of the numbers in the first grade. I think lots of teachers don't teach math to kids as they should. They waste too much time when they should be doing math in the lower grades. By the time my students leave my class in the sixth grade, they should be ready for algebra. But that can't happen unless the teachers in the earlier grades know what needs to be done. So for my geometry project I'm figuring out what needs to be taught when. I'm not done with it yet, but I already know the title: "Curriculum by Chris."

Chapter 22

ક્ષ·

Final Notes
Options (Carmen's thoughts—May 4)

T hings have really changed since I turned in my geometry project. I knew I could get a good grade on it because I got to choose what to write about. I wrote it like I write my stories, only this time I was the main character completely. Actually, there was only one character. First I did all the research, and then I became Albert Einstein. It took me six libraries and dozens of books, but I did it. I wrote the whole report from Einstein's point of view.

And it's not as if I couldn't relate to him, because he wasn't successful in school and he thought differently than the others. And he was creative, like me. He was smarter than I am, but I could handle most of that by reading what he'd said. I couldn't understand everything, but I understood enough to get inside of him and write my/his project.

The story was great. So good it didn't even matter too much if Mr. Healy liked it or gave me a good grade on it because I wrote it mostly for me. I think all projects and reports should be like that, then people would do a better job.

But the information about Einstein didn't stop when I turned in the project. It went a lot further than I ever imagined it would go. Not only did Mr. Healy give me a ninety-six for the project (which didn't hurt my grade at all), but I became the class expert on things beyond the third dimension. In the last couple of weeks, the groups in the class spent time looking at the fourth dimension with time and space travel. It was on a very simple level, fortunately, because every time there was a question, I was the authority they consulted. I was like an encyclopedia for the entire class. I stayed after class nearly every day with some of the people in the class. We talked about things that I couldn't have been more uninterested in last summer, but now I was the authority.

Because of my "expertise" in the area, I was not in a group; I was like a walking reference book. The first group I worked with was really involved in what Einstein calls a "mind experiment." They understood that if you accelerate a person to the speed of light, their time frame changes. I explained, if you take a rocket ship and send it out into space at the speed of light for two weeks, the person in the rocket ship would have aged two weeks, while the people here on earth would be three and a half years older. From that they did the following experiment.

Suppose we put Patty on a rocket ship and send her at the speed of light into space for two weeks. When she stops, she sees a phone booth and calls her friend Alicia back home. Alicia has gone through the rest of her high school years while Patty was gone for two weeks (Patty time).

"Hi, Alicia, it's me, Patty. What's going on back there?"

"Things have been so busy. Ever since I began at Stanford, I haven't had a minute to relax." And so on.

The thing that really bothered them wasn't that time had changed. It was that Patty would still be a junior, while Alicia, who is a freshman in our class, had gone past her.

Patty wanted to know how to reverse the process and return to earth. Their mind experiment didn't stop there. The next question they asked was: If you could reverse the time change process, would Alicia still get the phone call from Patty three and a half years later? It was perfect, because that's the sort of mind experiment Einstein did all the time. I tried to think just like he would, and come up with an answer, but I never did. Either Einstein didn't cover this or I didn't remember it, but it was fun to try to think like I figured he would.

The possibility of reversing the process came from another group, who recalled an investigation from a few months ago about how dimensions get changed. If you took a side off a three-dimensional figure like a cube you get a two-dimensional figure—a square. If you take a side off a square you get a one-dimensional figure—a line. If you take a side (well, an end) off a line you get a zero-dimensional figure—a point. Here comes the tricky part. If you could take a side off a point you'd be in the negative first dimension.

After that, you just follow the pattern. So if you took off another side, you'd be in the negative second dimension; again, and you'd be in the negative third dimension. If you did it one more time, you'd be in the negative fourth dimension. According to this group, the negative fourth dimension is used to reverse time travel. So to retrieve that rocket ship that was only two weeks gone while the earth had gone three and a half years, all you'd need to do is travel in the negative fourth dimension back to the present. Pretty neat, huh?

Even if it's totally unrealistic, we came up with it ourselves. That's what happens when you're able to think and use mind experiments. And when no one is there to tell you that you're wrong.

Boy, I sure wish I could use that negative fourth dimension to go backwards and change my grade in this class. I failed the first semester, but thanks to Albert Einstein I may pass this semester. If I could go back now and retake this class, things would be different. I know I could do it now.

I'm not going to worry about it, though, because I am already planning for the future. I spoke with my counselor and told her I want to take Geometry again this summer at Rio Hondo College so I can take Algebra II next year here at Mountain View. Some of my smart friends have taken classes at Rio Hondo, but until now I always thought college classes were for other people. I think I'm as smart as anyone else, it's just that I express it differently. Like in the report I did. I really worked hard to find out about Einstein, but it was fun work and worth the time. Even Edmund and Alicia were coming to me asking me questions they didn't know the answers to. It sure builds a person's confidence when that sort of thing happens.

The other thing that helped build my confidence happened nearly a month ago, when we were working with the Chris Shape. That's a funny-shaped pyramid that Chris came up with. Some of us were trying to figure out its volume. I thought the first thing we should do was measure the volume, then find some way of getting that number using the dimensions of the Chris Shape. However, the rest of my group disagreed with my method, so I helped them with their idea. But I couldn't get my idea out of my head. So I went my science teacher and asked her how she would go about it. Her method was exactly like mine. When I asked her how she'd measure the volume, she told me she had some special sand in her classroom that was used just for finding volumes.

The next day I took my new information to the group. They were enthusiastic and agreed to try it. Mr. Healy gave us permission to go to the science department to make the measurement. It turned out that while we were doing that, another group had brought plastic and tried to measure the volume by using water. A third group had figured it out using just a combination of Chris Shapes and a little imagination. We turned in our answers and the next day Mr. Healy announced that we'd all gotten the same results—which meant we had validated each other's experiments. We had all done our own thing and each group had done something different, but each of us had been successful.

Being successful, that's what this class has been for me beyond anything else. Whether it was the time I changed people's minds about the circle group Larry was leading, or the story that I have almost finished that Mr. Healy told me he really likes, writing about Einstein, or working together to find solutions, this class has been about successes for me. Even if I don't pass Geometry, I learned something more valuable in this class than anything that has to do with geometry. I found out that a person's success is less determined by the attitude of the world than I ever knew. Success is determined by your attitude towards the world, and I know I'm going to be successful no matter what happens.

Spinning Geometry (Larry's thoughts—May 24)

There it was for anyone to see, but no one's looking at it except for Enoch, Gerardo, Shawn, and me. Some guy has done the Pythagorean Theorem, but instead of squares on the sides of the triangles like Edmund had, the guy used half circles filled with liquid. So when you tilt the right triangle, the liquid from the two smaller semicircles fills the largest one completely. It was incredible.

We were with the entire band on our annual trip to National City for the Band Festival. They take us to some museum and we find this demonstration. We were really excited about it. Shit, the way we were reacting, you'd have thought we won the lottery. But it was out-standing, absolutely outstanding.

It started me thinking about the implications of this No Book geometry class that we're in. This thing hasn't taught us all there is to know about geometry, but it's enough to get by and it's made us inter-ested in things we had no interest in before. Shit, I can't believe the disagreements we've had over things that the people in the other classes never heard of. Last semester Sergio said, "In this class you make enemies out of friends by arguing over things that you wouldn't have even thought about last summer."

When he said that, I really enjoyed it because I like to argue. But now things have changed, for me at least. Now I enjoy investigat-ing and finding out more about things. I can look into things I really want to think about and I have people around to help me investigate. Yes, I said "help me." I'm usually still the leader of the group I'm in, but the rest of the people are now able to come up with ideas on their own and I... well, we help develop the ideas.

Spinning geometry is a perfect example. That's when you take a two-dimensional shape and spin it to become a three-dimensional object. It was originally Alicia's idea, but everyone in our group worked on it. Enoch was the one who said it had to be spun in the right way. Sergio figured that it had to do with the axis you spin it on. (We had trouble with the axis idea, so we gave it to another group to work on.) I said we'd need to experiment to determine if it works for all shapes. And Healy got us the cardboard and scissors to try it. I'm not saying we invented anything that would shock the world, but we did it by working together and everyone contributed to it.

Every group needs a leader and that's what I do best. If the group is to approach its maximum potential, everyone has to contrib-ute ideas and the leader must make the necessary decisions. Each person has equally good ideas, of course, but without the right leadership, the group is dust.

I've been in a couple of groups this year that didn't work out very well. Everyone has to do their job, and sometimes I didn't feel like doing mine. I know it wasn't exactly right, but I deserve the time to kick back every once in a while.

Enoch, Gerardo, Shawn, and I were kicking back on the beach during the band trip and we started talking about the times we spent at Band Camp each summer. Then we started talking about Geometry Camp again. We'd run it like we do our class, only this one could have more computers than the one crummy one we had to wait in line for whenever we wanted to use it. That bugged the shit out of me. And we could have things like the semicircle Pythagorean Proof there and all sorts of supplies so people could really look at things and experiment. I think a big part of our creativity was lost because we didn't have what we needed to build what we wanted.

As we were talking about the mythical Geometry Camp, I realized that these guys really are my friends. That we are going to graduate in a few weeks. And that I am going on to bigger and better things. I'd already decided sometime back in April that I am going to college. Actually, just to a junior college, to see if I like it. It won't cost much. I can live at home and even work on the side if I want.

Enoch, Gerardo, and Shawn didn't know it then, but I decided that day on the beach that they were going on with me. Heck, I don't know if there could ever be better friends out there than these guys. We don't just share D and D, band, and geometry—we share our ideas, our jokes, and our feelings with each other.

It's not like me to worry about the other guy. I used to figure that if a person can't take care of himself, who cares?

In that geometry class I learned who cares—me, that's who. Don't get me wrong, I still think people should take care of themselves, but everyone needs assistance sometimes.

I was drowning the day of that Metric Circle presentation. Then Carmen, who I thought was a nobody, rescued me. She had the courage to help because she saw me in trouble. Alicia rescued the whole class from drowning in Healy's incredible disorganization. When someone needs help, it's everyone's responsibility to give assistance in any way they can. They've (well, we've) all learned a lot, and not just geometry. And it's all just because I once said, "and this year in geometry, we're not going to use books."

Using the "Real Book" (Alicia's thoughts—June 5)

It's done, it's really done! Regardless of all that went wrong in that geometry class, yesterday we got the final edition of our geometry book. We titled it a word the whole class coined up. We call it, "Geometree." On the cover we have a picture of a family tree. It begins with a single point, that's the zero dimension. Then it continues to different dimensions and fans out to all the subsections of geometry. I thought it was a little corny, but it was finally done.

No more organization, no more holding my breath that Mr. Healy hasn't lost something vital, and no more inputting. The last two weeks trying to get all twenty-five pages transferred to the Macintosh so it could be laser printed with good graphics was really hard. I guess it was my perfectionism coming out again. I spent all my free time before and after school inputting information, but it was worth it. The final edition looked almost professional.

During the last two weeks before finals, Mr. Healy said we could use the class time to study for the final geometry exam. It made sense, seeing as we couldn't make any changes in our book. I asked if we had any chance of doing well on the final. I wanted to know if the people who used the textbooks were going to have a big advantage. Typically, he said he had no idea. I couldn't believe what I did next. I heard it coming out of my mouth, but I still couldn't believe it.

I said, "It's not fair that the other classes get to use real books and we can only study the useless book we coined up." I didn't really mean it like it sounded. It's not that I believe we're stupid, but how do we know? This class is one of the most important classes in high school. I just couldn't take a chance.

After he thought about it for a minute he said, "This class has been an experiment all year long. Why stop at this point? I never considered using anything but our book, but I understand your concern. I truly believe you can do as well with your 'Geometree' book as with any other book, but I can't blame you for questioning. It's your grade. You should decide for yourselves. So think about it tonight. Tomorrow I'll have copies of the text we used last year and the new one that the other classes are using this year. You let me know which book you want to use to study for the final."

I knew I'd caught him unprepared. If I'd known what I was going to say, I would have asked him after class, not in front of the whole class. But either way, it was something that had to be asked.

So, the next day we came in and chose what book we would use to study for our final. Ten people chose the old geometry book, twelve people chose the new book, and eleven people decided to use just our book. I chose the new book because I really want an even chance with my brother. I know we'll compare grades and I don't want him putting down the No Book class.

You know, I'm defensive about it, even if I'm not sure of the knowledge we gained. For me it was the best possible introduction to high school because it got me involved with people—not just the

freshmen that graduated from the other junior highs, but the sopho-
mores, juniors, and seniors that were already here. And I didn't just sit
there with them, I interacted with them. Plus, they all relied on me for
the information to be put in the book.

At first I thought they were making me responsible for what
went into the book, but that wasn't it. They were responsible for the
discoveries, and they wanted to make sure they got into the book. If I
hadn't done it, someone else would have. We started with three given
facts and it was totally our responsibility to create our book. Despite
the problems, we did it. No one will know the final results of the No
Book class until after we are gone. I do know that we took blank
pages and filled them with more than I would ever have guessed.
We'll find out on the final how much geometry we learned. But regardless of the amount of geometric knowledge, we learned to take
on responsibility that none of us ever expected. And you know, I'm
proud of ourselves.

What's It Mean? (Edmund's thoughts—June 10)

Some people say I'm crazy to spend time reviewing just our
"Geometree" book for the final, but I think I owe it to the class to do it
this way. If I study only our book, everyone else will have faith in it. I
know what we have developed isn't what my brothers studied when
they took geometry in high school, but it's all ours. It's not some other
author's opinion of the way geometry should be.

I want to get a good grade on the final and I want to get another A in this class. But this class gave me something I could never
have gotten without it—friends.

Before, if I had any friends, they were always just the smart
people, no matter what school I was at. The teachers always liked me,
and that's still true. But now when I walk around school I have friends

in the band, I have friends on the football team, I have friends in just about everything.

In the past everyone called me a "school-boy," but this year they call me a fifth-dimension thinker. I like that a whole lot better. After this class I know that even though I may think on a different level sometimes, I can communicate with any other people. People still make fun of me sometimes, but it's no longer with them laughing at me on one side and me being alone on the other. Now I can laugh at myself with the others and it's okay.

I didn't realize the improvement until after my presentation of the Park Proof—it sounds good just to say it. My communication problems and my decision to think for myself isolated me from other people. Either I never knew that before, or I was too scared to try to do anything about it. There's no isolation now. When I'm in the groups I talk, I laugh, I listen, and I work towards answers together with all the others. People listen to me and I listen to them. I want to share and learn with them. This is what communication is all about.

About the only thing I'm planning on doing by myself now is finding a way for the Park Proof to work algebraically. I know I can do it, I just haven't had a chance to sit down and write it out. Finding time for something like that used to be so easy. I had all the time in the world to think it out by myself, but now I have friends. So now the Park Proof will just have to wait until summertime.

A Final Look (Chris's thoughts—June 14)

Last year at this time, I was looking forward to being with my friends from Long Beach. But, even when I was planning it, I think I knew it wasn't going to happen. It's like I used to live my life hoping things would work but knowing deep down that there was no chance. For me there'd always be disappointment, just like last summer.

Not anymore though. Now I have a goal, and I have the ganas (that's Spanish for "desire," I got it from a movie I saw last weekend) to make things happen for me. The last school year has changed me so much that I will never see myself in the same way again. I am going to look for my opportunities to grow and help others. I always wanted to help other people, but I was so wrapped up in my own life and my own problems that I don't think I was much help to anyone, including myself. I'm looking forward to summer this year in a different way.

This may be my last summer at home if things work out with college and everything next year. As strange as it sounds, I'm planning on making this a family summer. I'm not going to be controlled by them, but I'm going to try and help them see how important communication and working together is. It may not work, but it doesn't have a chance unless someone tries. I saw it work in geometry class and in there we started with people who didn't know each other. I think it might work out better in my family. Letty and I are practically best friends and my brothers are more fun now than ever.

I wish there was some way for me to help open the communication between my parents. It would be so good for them. I don't think I've ever heard them just talk to each other. I have to work with them individually if I am going to have any effect.

Mom will be difficult, but I'm going to be as positive as I can with her. We've always had a "wait till your father gets home" relationship. We've never really dealt with each other. I'm going to continue to work and help out my mother, only now I'll work with her to do things. We'll be more like equals. We'll talk to each other and maybe we'll get to know each other.

The most difficult part will be with my dad. I used to think I hated him, but now I think I understand him better. The way he reacted while I was gone and since I've been back makes him seem like less of a threat and more of a human being. I know he isn't likely to change, and I know he feels he has lost control of me, but in losing control he has given me the chance to find out that I really love him. I know that he'll never be able to admit his mistakes to his own daughter; that's part of him. But I can try to build a relationship from my side even if he doesn't understand what's going on.

If I try to start a conversation about communication, he'll turn it into a control issue and try to win. He may try, but I will not be made to feel bad about myself anymore. I've done that for too long. I know that I am a worthwhile person and I know that my ideas are for real and are as valid as anyone else's. I believe in what I'm doing. I never really knew what I was doing before, but now I can think for myself and build my own future.

David tried to get me to look at my future, but I guess I wasn't ready to see it then. I really loved David. He tried so hard to get me to see what I was worth and gave me so much support. The reason I didn't get the message was because the only reason I did things was to see "that smile." The real miracle for me this year was learning that the positive response that really counts doesn't come from outside, it comes from within. If I'm ever going to be someone (and I am), it won't be to please anyone else. I'll do it for me.

Chapter 23

ৈ

The Bottom Line
(Chip's thoughts—June 20)

They're gone. The experimental No Book class is over. I can uncross my fingers, I can let out my breath. Saying good-bye to my students in June is never easy, but this year my empty classroom seems quieter than ever before. No more bigons, PLIT, or Park Proof. No more arguments over invisible geometry. Einstein is back in the history books, the Chris Shape is just a type of pyramid, and the Metric Circle is only an idea that was considered and discarded in a geometry class at Mountain View High School. For all the arguing and compromising and interacting caused by those topics, not a single one ended up in their book. No two-sided figures, Metric Circle, PLIT, or ducking lines. Invisible geometry was invisible in the final edition. The book was filled with twenty-five pages of definitions and Discovered Truths, but there was no place for the discarded items. Their "Geometree" book was good, but I have nothing to compare it to for evaluation.

However, now I can really evaluate the No Book class. All year I was determined to always be positive. I had to give the kids confidence with my attitude. I figured if I gave them no assistance other than to facilitate their progress and give the kids a picture of success, the results of the experiment would be legitimate.

The geometry finals from all the geometry classes have been corrected. The final test was a departmental test, not based on any particular text. It was a fair test of geometry knowledge, but the No Book class average remained five percent below the combined average of the other classes. We just couldn't make up the difference.

The final edition of "Geometree" was in their hands two weeks before the final. From that time on I let them use class time to study for the final. Some of the students were concerned about not having a "real" geometry book to study for the final. So I let the students choose if they wanted to study some of the other texts. One-third of the class chose last year's text. One-third chose the text the other classes had used this year. The remaining third used only our "Geometree" book. As it turned out, the averages of each of these three groups were virtually identical.

Edmund's score on the final was the highest not only in the class, but in the entire school as well. However, we also had some of the lowest scores. Alicia had one of the highest scores, but her brother still beat her by two points. Carmen received a D- on the final and a D in the class. She'll still have to take Geometry at Rio Hondo, if she wants to take Algebra II here next year. If it hadn't been for her project on Einstein and all the interest that evolved from her knowledge of Einstein, I'm sure she would have failed. Larry's C+ on the final was enough to pass Geometry, even if it was the spring semester of his senior year, which he always said was "kick back time." Chris had a B and passed the class second semester, but I still don't know if she got credit for first semester grades. I think Chris was one of the people who grew the most during this year. I'd like to think it was partly due to the No Book class. I think Chris will be a success now and go on to college, even if her first semester grades don't count. She may run up against obstacles in her future, but I think she's capable of handling nearly anything now. She's got the motivation and desire to succeed.

On the first day of school last fall there were twenty students registered in the No Book class. On the last day there were thirty-three. Twenty-five of the final thirty-three passed the class, which is a higher passing percentage than most of the past geometry classes I've taught. The success rate was higher than in the past, but neither that nor the grades on the final test tell the story of what happened in that class. It's the intangibles that count, not just the knowledge. It's what happened inside the individuals. They did learn to think, and their interest in geometry was intense. They learned to work together and come up with solutions to seemingly unsolvable differences. They learned to respect each other's opinions, and at the same time they seemed to grow stronger in their own commitment to things they felt were really important. They learned to express their feelings and thoughts. And they left this class with a new level of confidence in themselves. The positive effect on their self-esteem could never be measured, but I know it was there.

I think we were all just trying to survive at first. When a person is given a stiff challenge (like the No Book class) and is able to meet that challenge head-on and survive, the resulting increase in confidence and self-esteem is overwhelming. For me personally, this was an exceptional year for all my classes. The change wasn't in the No Book class itself as much as in the feeling I carried around inside and the way I approached all the classes regardless of their level.

It was the No Book class experience that convinced me to place the responsibility of learning on the students, from my lowest basic math classes to my algebra class to both geometry classes.

I learned that not knowing the answer was okay and that kids learn better sometimes if the teacher isn't the source of all knowledge.

The other thing the No Book class made me do was evaluate what really matters in my classes. I decided that grades aren't important; what's important is learning. People won't learn unless they accept the responsibility to learn. This isn't so earth shattering, but once I was released from the tyranny of grades I began to use them to make deals to influence the kids to take on the responsibility of learning.

"If everyone is in class tomorrow for the test, I'll give each of you five extra points."

"If you will give this class your best effort for the rest of the semester, I'll throw out all your previous failing scores."

"If the class average on this test is 80 percent or better, we'll skip the next test."

The students have to decide to take responsibility for their learning. It is my job simply to discover how that can best be accomplished. Then the learning will take care of itself.

So the No Book kids weren't the only ones who were changed; I was changed as well. I believe now that if you give people some time, a task, and motivation, they will create marvelous things. I knew about having time and a task, but the motivation for the No Book class still remains somewhat of a mystery. Was it the type of student that signs up for geometry? Was it just an unusual class, or would it work in any geometry class? There are so many questions that remain unanswered, but the message is clear: don't make us the only No Book class. The miracle works.

Chris saw the miracles long before I did, but I think she made one error in judgment. I wasn't creating the miracles, the kids were. In retrospect, I think that was always the real question—not could they, but would they decide to create miracles? Create they did, change they did. Each person was unique back in September when they entered the class, so each was affected differently by the class. But when they left they were all empowered by their experience.

This may have been the last day of school, but I don't believe the class is over. In fact, for many in that class, it is just the beginning. This class was just the first chapter. Their stories remain to be written.

Epilogue

In the years following the first No Book geometry class, the students of that original class continued to move forward. Meanwhile, the concept of No Book evolved into Build-A-Book and flourished.

Carmen failed the first semester of Geometry, but the experience of being in the No Book class gave her a confidence that was hard to deny. In her words, "I didn't like this class when it started and I hated math. In fact I was pretty pessimistic about a lot of things. I don't think I knew it then, but I know it was true. I think I changed a lot. This class changed a lot of things. We all learned to believe in ourselves and in each other. I don't hate math anymore, but I still don't really love it. And, you know, now I think I can handle just about anything in my life."

Carmen became empowered by the No Book class, and it changed her future. She found that she could do math and that there would never again be a stumbling block in her life like eights times tables had once been.

Due to her first-semester failure Carmen had to take Geometry again. It was not offered by Mountain View in summer school so she went to the local community college. Before No Book, she wouldn't have had the confidence to go to a junior college, but after the class her self-doubt vanished. At the junior college she adjusted quickly and easily got credit for Geometry. In her senior year at Mountain View, Carmen successfully completed Algebra II and went on to Cal State University at Fullerton after graduation. In retrospect, Carmen says it was during the No Book class that she decided to attend college. She is majoring in business administration and plans to organize a group of people from business to help poor people. She still thinks she can change the world—maybe she can.

Alicia with her "photogenic memory" (it always struck me as peculiar that with all her brilliance she confused photogenic and photographic, but it was somehow consistent with her personality) was very successful in her high school years, and she no longer had to worry about keeping one of her teachers organized. Her GPA at graduation, three years after No Book, was slightly below 4.0. She passed AP Calculus as a junior and BC Calculus as a senior. She entered the University of California at Berkeley in the fall after she graduated.

As for Edmund, in the summer following the No Book class he algebraically proved the Park Proof of the Pythagorean Theorem. His algebraic proof was based on the original drawing of the Park Proof. His final version of the Park Proof was not only valid, it was a new proof of the Pythagorean Theorem and was published in the Journal for Mathematical Behavior. It took him nearly a full semester in Algebra II to adjust to using a textbook for math again, but he continued and finished with an A. Edmund completed Calculus in his senior year. His creative writing was much admired at Mountain View.

He went to Pomona College with a plan to major in electrical engineering.

Larry and his friends graduated that spring and entered Mount San Antonio College in the fall, where they all tested out of taking any further geometry classes (though they failed the algebra section). They have differing goals but continued more or less together until they finished at Mount San Antonio College. After "keeping his options open," Larry went to work for a bank.

Chris was not as successful academically as the others. The next fall, problems at home once again forced her to leave. She moved in with her boyfriend's sister, but this time she kept in contact with her entire family. Her father made several unsuccessful attempts to force her to return home. He then contacted the police and threatened to have her placed in a foster home until she was eighteen.

Meanwhile, Chris's boyfriend had asked her to marry him several times, but she had turned him down each time. Her plans didn't include marriage for some time, but her father's threat changed the timing and Chris married her boyfriend to avoid her father's final effort to control her.

Ironically, Chris felt she had avoided being controlled by her father, and yet his threats had caused her to run away twice and then to get married before finishing high school. His struggle for control may not have changed his daughter as he had planned, but his actions had a definite effect on her future plans.

In the next few years, Chris bore two children, received her high school diploma, was hired as a teacher's aide in an elementary school, and, the control issue no longer applicable, began to rebuild her relationship with her father. With her new status as a parent and with the help of her sister, Letty, Chris and her father have repaired their relationship and become friends.

And Chris is more determined than ever to become an elementary school teacher. Nearly five years after her No Book experience, she was able to take the next step. The school district in which she was employed as an aide recognized her unique skills with young people and her self-confidence. The district all but guaranteed her a job as a teacher when she completed her schooling, and they offered to assist her financially. The road will not be smooth, but she is enrolled in Chaffey Community College and has begun the process. It may be slow, but can there be any doubt that this determined young lady will be creating miracles in her own future classroom?

As for the No Book class, it began again with new faces the following fall. This time I knew that the result would be a student-created book, so the name was changed to Build-A-Book, but the format and intentions remained the same. The names and personalities of the students were different and the three given facts weren't exactly the same, but basically the results were similar. And the students were equally successful in all the immeasurable ways the original class had been. The big difference the second year in the Build-A-Book class was the test score comparison. We didn't have the highest score in the school on the final, nor the lowest, but the class average was higher by five percent than that of any other geometry class in the school. And all but one Build-A-Book student got at least a C on the comprehensive final taken by all the geometry students.

Certainly the success in future mathematics courses is a good indication that those who take BAB are equipped to go on in mathematics. And there has been much success mathematically, but such intangibles as increased confidence and self-esteem, and the ability to work with others, to solve problems, and to think creatively, had no scale on which to be measured until two or three years later. Then I began to notice how many former Build-A-Book students there were in student government and on the Academic Decathlon team. I did a little investigation and came up with the following statistics, which seem to validate the assumption that taking a BAB class changes students' lives and affects them far beyond the classroom door.

In the first four years of BAB there were a total of five BAB classes, involving 150 students out of the 3600 students who have attended Mountain View during that time period. In those four years

- Forty-four percent of the Academic Decathlon team members were former BAB students.
- Twenty-four percent of the contributors to Voices, the literary magazine, were former BAB students.
- Twenty-three percent of the people running for student-body office were former BAB students.
- Thirty-three percent of the students considered for the next year's Academic Decathlon team were former BAB students.
- Nineteen percent of the AP Calculus class were BAB students. (Five of the six freshmen in the original No Book class completed at least one year of Calculus.)
- Twenty percent of the student newspaper staff were former BAB students.
- Sixteen percent of the student-body presidents were former BAB students.

This is pretty convincing evidence that Build-A-Book has far reaching effects that go beyond mathematics.

Appendix 1

ઽ&·

The Format of the Build-A-Book Class

I left the classroom for a year to write *Creating Miracles* in the hope that the information in this book would help more teachers realize the need for risk taking and give them the courage to experiment. There are many avenues for the risk taker to travel, and Build-A-Book is but one. This appendix includes an in-depth explanation of the Build-A-Book class for teachers of any subject to read and internalize for their own growth. When a teacher decides to begin taking risks, this section may be a source of support and understanding.

The following format was written after four years of experimenting with the Build-A-Book approach, and it will contain some insight not found in the rest of the book. I have discovered in that time that I have had to adjust my approach each year, depending on the make-up of the class. The following information reflects some of those changes.

If you should choose to do a similar experiment, it is important that you develop the class to suit your own personal style of teaching. No two Build-A-Book classes will be the same. Each class will differ because each teacher is unique and the personalities of the students in each class are different. It is the students who ultimately determine the direction and focus of the class.

The most important thing to remember is that the students creating this curriculum have been given a monumental task. They need large doses of support and positive feedback from the teacher.

In our class, the desks are positioned together in groups of four, creating a group working space in between. This arrangement of desks, with few exceptions, remains the same throughout the year. Individual groups or people may move desks around to facilitate their investigations at any time. For myself, I have the groups of desks arranged unevenly on a diagonal (the front of the room is the northeast corner), because I want the students to know from the moment they enter that they are in an unusual classroom.

On the first day, I am at the door as they come in, randomly dividing them into groups using a deck of cards. If there are thirty-six students, I take the deck of cards and remove all the cards higher than nines. On each group of desks is a card with a number one through nine. Those students whom I hand a four as they enter sit in a desk of the four group, and so on. There are many other techniques of arranging students randomly, but this is how I have done it.

After the generic first day's introduction and dissemination of information, I inform the class that they will not be using a text and must develop the subject matter for themselves. I am very positive about their ability to undertake such a task, and I am careful to show confidence that if Euclid could develop geometry thousands of years ago, they can do the same today.

Next I explain that I will give them three geometric facts to start with and nothing further. I suggest they get out a piece of paper and write down these three given facts. In each class the students have been so astonished at the announcement of creating their own curriculum that they readily take out paper to write down any geometric knowledge I give them. Then I explain that from now on they must decide as a class what facts are valid and what are not.

After this I explain the idea of working in groups, that each individual in the group is important and that all of them must contribute for the success of the class. Next, I tell each group to pick a person to write down all the things that are discussed on the paper they are about to be handed. After a space for all four names on the sheet of paper, called an investigation sheet, there is one of the three given statements. Under that the word Responses is written, followed by an empty sheet of lined paper which they will fill in with the dialogue and ideas that come out of their group work. (A sample investigation sheet is found in Appendix 2.)

Day 1 Group Work

Each group receives an investigation sheet with one of the three given facts on it. If there are thirty six in the class, that means that three groups will have the same given fact to discuss. I try not to give the same statement to groups right next to each other. The first year I used these given facts:

> Parallel lines never meet.
>
> A triangle contains 180 degrees.
>
> A linear pair contains 180 degrees. (I used a picture, not the term linear pair.)

In succeeding years I have tried:

> A parallelogram contains 360 degrees.
>
> A circle contains 360 degrees.
>
> Non-parallel lines meet.
>
> Alternate interior angles are equal. (Once again, I used a picture.)

Each year I included information about parallel lines and degrees in a three-or four-sided figure, but the third fact varied. However, another teacher who tried BAB in a different school began with the assumptions of Euclid's *Elements* and found that to be a successful point of departure.

My instructions to the students are purposely minimal. I want them to understand the limited teacher direction. And I want them to begin to accept responsibility for their learning as soon as possible.

On the first day, the groups have handed in investigation sheets that are nearly full. I think there are a variety of reasons for the completeness of the sheets. The academically-oriented students, who were worried about "gaining enough knowledge," participated in order to make as much they could out of this situation. The students who came in fearing geometry participated because they found they had a chance to be involved without fear of failing. And the students in the class that were repeating geometry were treated as special by the class because they had studied "real" (make that "traditional") geometry. All the students were confused by the actions of the teacher and didn't know what to expect next.

Each year the responses of the first day vary widely. Different groups take different directions. Some groups may be talking about the unusual class, others are finding out about each other, but all groups spend some time wrestling with the given statement. Listed below are a few examples of the kind of responses the students make on that first investigation sheet:

If the parallel lines never meet, then they don't cross.

Parallel lines are sexy.

The universe goes on and on so parallel lines must go on and on.

Parallel lines can and can't be the same distance apart.

What if a parallel line breaks or becomes defective?

A triangle has three angles.

A linear pair looks like a y on its side.

A rainbow does not meet in a reflection of itself.

Are you Chinese? I love Chinese food, but my mother can't cook it.

The number of degrees in a triangle depends on its shape.

A circle has to be measured different than other figures.

These statements determine the direction for the next day's investigation sheets. That night I read all the investigation sheets and underline the most interesting statements. I pick some statements that are geometry related and others that are not because I want the students to be aware that all their comments have worth. I choose the next day's investigation sheet topics from the underlined statements.

Day 2

At the start of the second day, I always compliment the class on their first day's work. Then I read selected comments. I include some of the remarks that were not geometry related and explain that all communication is worthwhile, even if it's just to get to know the members of your group. Then I hand out the investigation sheets for the day with the same instructions as the previous day. I make an effort to give each group a new statement each day, not one they created the previous day. (For example, Group One will not get a topic from the sheet Group One turned in the day before.)

During the class I try to visit as many groups as possible and comment on their effort. The personal positive interaction validates the overall positive statements I make at the beginning of each class. I try to see the possibilities in every idea and comment on them.

The length of responses on the second and following days on each investigation sheet varies tremendously. It is helpful to keep reminding them to write down everything said in the groups.

The Daily Tasks

Each day's investigation sheets were determined by the work of the previous day.

The first year I had only one computer in the classroom (by the fourth year we had six Apple Macintoshes™). It was available to any group that requested it. That year we used *The Geometric Supposer* distributed by Sunburst which does pretty much what its name suggests. We used three disks: Triangles, Quadrilaterals, and Circles. The students made conjectures about what they were investigating and then used the *Supposer* to draw the figures accurately and measure any dimensions. This technology allowed the students to progress at a rate Euclid could never have imagined.

In 1990, *The Geometer's Sketchpad* from Key Curriculum Press became available to my students. It is an outstanding piece of software for the Macintosh that lets students draw shapes and maneuver them on the screen. It allows the creativity of the students to flourish. *The Geometer's Sketchpad* is an excellent piece of software and I felt sure it would replace the *Supposer* in popularity in my classroom, but my students again proved me wrong. With both programs available to them they were somehow able to determine which software would be most useful for their needs at any given time. I found that they used both programs frequently, but didn't have a preference for one program over the other.

As the year continued, my role became that of a facilitator. I gave my opinions (which were considered no more valuable than one of the student's opinions), located supplies, offered suggestions, and asked questions. I worked very hard not to ask leading questions, but merely questions that were for my own clarification or my own curiosity. (Example: What does a negative dimension look like?)

Homework

For the first semester the homework assignments are frequent, but may not be every night. They consist mostly of definitions. Since I don't introduce vocabulary as part of the class, the students must determine it. This begins early each year when a group questions the meaning of a word on an investigation sheet. I write that word down in my notebook, as well as any words I hear questioned by any group or after class when students ask me questions. When I have more than three such words I assign the definitions for homework. I tell the students they can get definitions from the dictionary, a geometry book, friends, family, or they can create their own—the most frequent method.

The homework in the second semester varies widely. It can be proving that certain thoughts are valid, or rewriting ideas or definitions when questions arise. It just depends on the class and what they are doing during class time.

Although the homework assignments are not as consistent or of the same kind as a traditional textbook-run class might be, one of the most incredible results of this class happens outside, where many of the students take their free time after school, before school, on weekends, and over vacations investigating geometric possibilities.

The Road from Question to Class Definition

The day after a vocabulary homework assignment I stand at the door as the students enter and collect the assignments. (Actually, after a month or so I have a student collect the homework at the door.) Then I choose a group to take all of these definitions and derive for each word a single definition that they feel is the one closest to the consensus of the class. The consensus definitions are handed in on an investigation sheet. I take them and write them in my book to be kept for the following week.

On Monday the normal investigation sheet approach is suspended if there have been several consensus definitions from the previous week. These words and their definitions are put on the board and discussed. When there is disagreement, the class reworks and rewords until they come up with a definition they can agree on. Some Mondays the class discussions are short; other times they take nearly the entire time.

The agreed-upon definitions become part of the class's book, which is kept on a word processor. I have a student in charge of inputting things into the computer. (The person doing the input may be changed randomly.)

One of the most difficult things for a teacher is allowing the students to make mistakes with their definitions (Euclid probably wasn't perfect the first time either) and not correcting them. Despite the difficulty that this presents, I believe it is absolutely necessary. A colleague of mine began a BAB class, and things went well until one day in the end of October when he tried to correct an error in the students' logic. The teacher's frustration simply reached a point where he felt action had to be taken. However, the class viewed his intervention as the opportunity to get a glimpse of "real" geometry. This correction revealed to the students the way to coerce their teacher into giving them geometric facts. The class would purposely make an error and the teacher would correct them with knowledge from traditional geometry. The class had transferred the responsibility for learning back to the teacher. That BAB class ended at the close of the first semester.

If left uninterrupted, the students will eventually produce solid definitions. The following is the metamorphosis of a definition from September until its final wording in April:

> Line—the path of a moving point. (9/19)
>
> Line—the exhaust of a moving point. (12/2)
>
> Line—a mark made up of dots connected to one another, starting at one point, extending in any direction and ending wherever you want it to end. (12/13)
>
> Line—a continuous straight path of connecting points. (4/11)

Frequently, the students decided their definitions needed changes. They discovered weaknesses as they explored further thoughts and concepts. By June the final definition was usually similar to Euclid's. (How long did it take him to reach certain conclusions?)

How "Discovered Truths" Become Discovered

Discovered Truths become part of the book in different ways. Sometimes when I am walking around during the course of a class, I see something in a group that I think would make a good presentation. In that case I ask the group if they would be interested in presenting it to the rest of the class. I am careful not to just ask for presentations from groups determining truths of my internal geometry. Anything that looks well developed and would be of interest to others in the class is a candidate for presentation. The group members then decide among themselves if it is something they would like to present.

Other times groups approach me about something they think is significant that their group has isolated. They request to present it to the class and we work together to determine the best time.

Occasionally an individual has found something he or she thinks is important for the class to know about. The individual discoveries can be as valid as any group discoveries. Usually the individual talks to me about a presentation before or after class.

The process from that point is fairly similar. I talk to the presenter(s) and request that for their own sake they have the thing they want to present in an organized, orderly fashion, and that they understand what they have discovered and are ready to answer all questions. This talk is frequently ignored in the beginning and the presentation is flawed, but the discoveries and the arguments in favor of it become stronger with each presentation. Each presentation must be defended against all the questions and arguments from fellow class members, which is a major factor in the improvement of the presentations over time.

As always, there are no rules about presentations. Some have included charts, some have had handouts, some presenters have required the entire class to participate by leaving the room and going to a specific location for the presentation.

After the presentation there is time for questions, discussions, arguments, and changes, and finally a vote is usually taken. Again, there are no absolutes. Sometimes the class or a vocal individual requests that more research be done and the presentation be repeated in the future. If a vote is taken and it passes, the presented fact is input into the computer and becomes part of their book.

It should be noted that a definition or Discovered Truth may be put in the book for a period of time and removed if there is a flaw found in it later in the year.

The Building of the Book

The first book in late September or early October is usually only a page or two, and includes only given facts and definitions.

About every two weeks I take their book as it is and get a printout. I generate enough copies for everyone in the class.

Information in the book constantly changes. New information is added, sometimes old information is deleted, and frequently there are definitions and Discovered Truths that need updating. This freedom to make changes means I have always been unable to just run off the "new" information and have them add it to their book.

The work of creating new books is done every two or three weeks. In the beginning it isn't hard, but by spring it is a real project, with thirty-six copies of twenty-page books to be run off and collated.

Tests

When I started the BAB concept, testing was the only place I could see that I would really have the opportunity to have an influence on the proceedings in the class. However, this didn't materialize as I had imagined.

I usually give the students about a week's notice of an upcoming test, which takes place every two or three weeks. Two days before the test I make sure they are all given a copy of the latest edition of the book. One day before the test I give them the entire day to review their book as a class. This process is usually student led but can be teacher led. It is the class's opportunity to eliminate ambiguities or hard-to-understand elements of their book.

Before the class I usually ask for a person to make a copy for me with all the changes the class makes during the review day. It is important to the students that I have exactly the same copy as they have, because I make up the test from the book I am given and the correct answers will be taken from that book.

That night I read over their book with the changes and underline things that I think are: (1) extremely well done and I want to commend, (2) definitions and Discovered Truths that I believe they don't really either understand or believe in, or (3) errors they left in the final copy of the book.

Those are the things I test them on. I use three methods of testing. The Sometimes, Always, Never statements are routinely the toughest. The Fill in the Blanks sentences I use to point out typos and questionable definitions. And the explanations are simply paragraph proofs of the Discovered Truths. The students usually do best on the Explanation section. Later in the year I usually add a section I call Extensions. This section uses the knowledge they have gained to solve certain real-life problems.

I encourage them to explain why they have answered a question the way they did on the Sometimes, Always, Never section and on the Fill in the Blanks section. These explanations are written in the space around the question.

The day after the test I return the results (routinely very poor, especially in the beginning) and we go over them. I give them my reasoning for the answers I have, and if there are questions we discuss them. Sometimes the students change my mind and the entire class gains back some points, but not very often.

Below are the same sample questions from the first semester's test that appeared in Chapter 16, but in this section I have added explanations for the answers.

Sometimes, Always, Never

10._____ Space is area.

11._____ The endpoints of a line are congruent.

12._____ Lines are always straight.

13._____ A line segment in a hexagon that was drawn from the center of one side to the center of another side is parallel to one side.

14._____ A point has no length or width so it is invisible.

15._____ Any two angles in a parallelogram are either congruent or supplementary.

Reasoning

Each of the following explanations was according to the book they gave me when I created the test.

10. (S) Their book definition at the time was Space—the area or region of everything.

11. (A) All points are congruent.

12. (A) At this point their definition of line said "straight."

13. (A) Their definition of hexagons described only regular hexagons.

14. (S) It may have depth and therefore could be visible.

15. (A) This statement was testing one of their best definitions.

Fill in the Blanks

32._____ A statement that can be validated with logical reasoning.

33._____ =

34._____ Parallel lines intersected by a third line.

35._____ _____ are angles that add up to 90 degrees.

32. (Proven Fact)   33. (Circumference)   34. (Parasector)

35. (Complimentary Angles)

Answers (Reasoning in parentheses)

32. Proven Fact (Clear and easy answer)

33. Circumference (In their book was the word "Circumference = " not followed by a definition, and it went unchecked the previous day)

34. Parasector (Simply their word for two lines cut by a transversal)

35. Complimentary Angles (must be spelled with an "i" not "e" to be marked correct, since this is how they spelled it in their book)

This was the first test on which Alicia earned an A. The questions on the test are difficult and sometimes misleading, but it serves as a good review of the edition of the book from which the test questions were taken. It seems sensible that question 33 would be one that the class would remedy as soon as they possibly could, but in the case of "Circumference" it took them three tests to finally write a definition for the word. I mention this to demonstrate that the teacher can use a test to indicate the things he or she thinks needs work, but cannot be assured that the students will reevaluate their book.

Groups

I have experimented with groups several times. As the year progresses things can be changed with less and less disruption. I have changed the group size from two to eight members and have met with mixed success.

One year I had a group each week in the spring be the "editing" group. Their task was simply to review the book and question the validity or clarity of the information. These questions could become investigation sheets, or the editing group might choose to investigate the issue themselves. They would also evaluate the new information before it entered the book. The concept met with varied success. Some two-week periods the group doing the editing would be totally absorbed in the process, but other weeks were not very successful. The process of editing must take a certain mix of personalities to work effectively.

For a couple of months one year I had a group whose sole job was to take the investigation sheets and read and evaluate them for the next day's investigation sheets. That way the class could be totally self-run. The idea had some merit and worked moderately well. The major problem was that it meant that on the first Tuesday they had nothing to do. On Wednesday they evaluated Tuesday's work and returned investigation sheets from Tuesday assignments to the groups on Thursday. And on Thursday the evaluation group read and created investigations sheets from Wednesday's work. In theory it could work, but in reality I just couldn't keep it organized. After a couple of different attempts I classified the experiment unsuccessful and returned to the original pattern.

What If?

We cannot leave this appendix without addressing the primary fear of all teachers: What if the class falls apart? It has happened to me twice in four years, out of a total of six classes. There are always better and worse days, and there are groups that seem to be progressing better on some days than others. Keeping in mind that the class changes randomly every two weeks is helpful if there is a group that is stagnant.

One spring, in the third BAB class I had, things fell apart. One Wednesday they came in and I handed out their investigation sheets and told them it was time to get started. Usually after that there is some superfluous talk, but the class begins after a few minutes. I am always uncomfortable in those minutes, because it always signals the possibility that the class might never get started. That fear had been unfounded until that day. For whatever reason, the class refused to begin. I sat and corrected papers. No luck. I left the room. When I returned they still had not begun.

At the end of the day investigation sheets were turned in blank. I tried to write this day off as an aberration, and fortunately I had a reserve of topics for the next day's investigation sheets. So the following day began without criticism or mention of the previous day, only positive words. But again nothing was done.

The next day I announced that I was proud of all they had done so far, but there were no new investigation sheets because nothing had been done the last two days. The class proceeded to sit and talk. They made no attempt to repair the situation. I didn't know what to do, so I did nothing. I corrected papers, did work for other classes, and left the classroom whenever I needed a break from the class. It was extremely difficult.

One thing that helped was that after a few days I had the feeling the class was trying to force me to take charge. I didn't know how to fix the class, but I did know that taking charge wasn't right.

This stalemate lasted twelve days. That's a long time to flounder—a long time for a teacher to wait. After twelve days a group came to me and asked me to leave the class alone for the entire class time the next day, which I did. The same group spoke to me after the day the class spent talking. They requested that I listen to all their gripes the next day without responding until everyone was heard.

So I sat in front of a large circle of desks and listened to their complaints. They were frustrated, because they felt they were getting cheated. After a full class period of complaints I told them I would respond the next day. At that time I reiterated the freedom they had in this class and the option to study other books outside of class time. I told them that the BAB format would continue and that I understood their fears, but that I was confident in their creative skills and abilities to discover geometry.

With the air cleared they returned to BAB and finished the year very successfully.

I also need to describe my fifth-period class in the year 1990-91. They were a dynamic class until Christmas break. By the end of the first semester their book was better than any other BAB book at the same time. I have no explanation, but at this point they ceased to function. And never recovered. I waited and worked with those who were most interested, but finally in May I gave up.

That BAB became a book class for the six weeks that remained in the year. It was frustrating for me, but the class was not a failure. In those six weeks we covered over half of the traditional text-book. That means that in a third of a year even an unsuccessful BAB class can cover the traditional course.

But it also indicated that there are no guarantees. Risk taking never becomes predictable or comfortable, just exciting for the teacher and positive for the students.

One aspect of the BAB student that has not been fully discussed in this book is the dedication to learning that this sort of subject creates. In *Build-A-Book Geometry*, Larry talks about a Geometry Camp. This sort of thought is not unusual; in fact, it is the norm. Chris's sister, Letty, became a BAB student and she once said, "The toughest thing about BAB is the lack of sleep. Each night I have trouble going to sleep because I am thinking about geometry and about how I am going to convince the people in my group."

Before and after school, at lunch, on weekends, and over vacations, BAB students wanted time to pursue theories and ideas.

I decided before the summer of 1990 that I would ask if there were BAB students interested in going Beyond BAB in the summer. I got such a response that I developed an application form. I chose twelve students (the BBAB was open to any BAB student present or past) for the program because I was allowed to hold it on the Cal State campus and I had only twelve spaces in my van.

I allotted them one week to experiment with BBAB. We met weekly through the rest of the school year and summer to arrange how we were going to approach the experience. I envisioned BBAB to be an hour a day, one-week course where I would be extraneous. In the end the students had determined the course to be six hours a day for two weeks. This is the sort of interest generated by BAB and how empowered the students feel.

The two weeks were not entirely smooth, and it was a real experiment, but on the final Friday the students were still working at 5:00—two hours after the BBAB was supposed to have finished.

BAB is not the total solution for education, but risk taking and finding new and different approaches comprise a major part of the solution. And it must begin in the classroom.

Appendix 2

≈⋆

From Conception to Presentation

T his appendix takes an idea all the way from its conception to its presentation and acceptance by the class. The BAB class represented here is the class that produced the book found in Appendix 3.

Names_____

Group 2

_____

Date January 12

_____

_____

Statement: A circle is made up of really small straight sides.

Responses:

1. Bernadette says this is a stupid statement.

2. How can a circle have straight sides? There aren't any straight sides to a glass when you drink out of it and it's a circle isn't it?

3. Brian says if it does have straight sides the sides must be so small you couldn't measure them.

4. But what if it was a really big circle?

5. Even if it was the earth, you couldn't see the small sides.

6. But Bernadette says the earth looks flat so maybe it's true.

7. Quynh-Anh thinks that circles are made up of arcs and she says that arcs are always curved.

8. All the people in Columbus' time thought the world was flat because it looked flat. Maybe they were looking at one of the straight parts. Maybe circles are made up of straight pieces.

9. This is dumb. We can't learn geometry this way.

10. Maybe arcs can be flat or maybe they can be barely curved.

11. Circles are curved lines.

12. We think only curved lines make arcs.

13. McDonald's has Golden Arches and they aren't straight.

14. A flat line can't be laid on a circle except if it touches it twice because the circle curves and the line doesn't.

15. Why can't the cafeteria at school get McDonald's food?

I took the paper and circled the ideas I thought had some interest or merit. In this case I circled numbers 7, 10, 12, 14, and 15. From this Tuesday investigation sheet I made investigation sheets for Wednesday with the following statements at the top:

Maybe arcs can be flat or maybe they can be barely curved.

Only curved lines make arcs.

Why can't the cafeteria at school get McDonald's food?

I saved numbers 7 and 14 for later.

It is important to me that they know that they could think about anything and record responses on things that weren't on the original investigation sheets, such as numbers 8, 9, and 13.

At the beginning of each day I usually talked for a few minutes about what was going on—either something in the class or outside the class that indicated the students were doing something special. This way I could give them some positive feedback as a whole group. After that time I either randomly handed out the sheets with the investigations at the top, or I put them in a basket in the rear of the class and had the groups retrieve their own.

The next day, I gave Group Four the investigation sheet with the statement "Only curved lines make arcs" (response 12 on Group Two's investigation sheet of Tuesday). On the investigation sheet below are the responses of Group Four to the statement:

Names_____

Group 4

_____

Date January 13

_____

_____

Statement: Only curved lines make arcs

Responses:

1. Not true, Noah made an arc.

2. What is an arc?

3. Sylvia said an "S" isn't an arc.

4. The rest of us don't agree.

5. Phoung thinks we should only consider parts of circles as arcs because it could get too confusing to consider things like "S".

6. Danny doesn't care.

7. Sylvia thinks you measure arcs with string—a yardstick wouldn't work because it's too straight.

8. Danny says a yardstick could work if you were real careful.

9. I don't think either way would be very accurate.

10. Phoung had this way of measuring with a protractor—then it would be in degrees. I like inches better. I even like centimeters better. Degrees change too much.

11. Sylvia can take any arc and find the circle it's part of and the center.

12. Then Danny connected the center and the ends of the arc and measured it with the protractor.

13. It may not be inches, but it does work and it's our idea.

After class on Wednesday, Group Four came and asked me if they could present what they had discovered to the entire class. They felt what they had discovered was worthy of entry into their book but knew it needed class approval. I told them they could prepare their presentation Thursday and present it to the class on Friday.

So Group Four spent Thursday in preparation. I try to get time to at least listen to a group's presentation while they are preparing it, but was unable to do so on this occasion. My presence doesn't appear to be necessary for the group, but it makes me feel better. The driving force in presentations is the need to explain things logically to their peers. In the past, the final authority has been the teacher reading a proof on a test and passing judgment on its validity. In BAB the evaluation comes from their classmates, who are ever so much more critical than the teacher. The teacher knows the direction and proper logic when reading a proof. The class has no idea what is being presented to them, and they are called upon to vote to determine if what was presented makes sense and should be a part of their book. If the presentation doesn't make sense, they don't want the discovery in their book. So Thursday's preparation was intense.

Not only is the logic in the presentation itself a concern, but perhaps even more important is the question-and-answer period that follows any presentation. Not only must the group prepare a logical explanation, they must be prepared to defend what they have discovered. Much of the preparation time is usually spent trying to imagine the questions that could be asked and developing responses to those questions.

Group Four decided for their presentation to illustrate their idea on poster board. This avoided one of the common pitfalls in BAB presentations: drawing the illustrations on the board. For whatever reasons, the "illustrate-as-you-prove" school of presentation causes problems. The kids are unfamiliar with the board and they tend not to be accurate with their drawings. The process can cause them to lose their train of thought. The drawn-on-the-spot pictures often raise unexpected questions from the class, which tend to remove the focus of the class from the discovery to be demonstrated. Group Four chose to avoid the board, and one member volunteered to spend the evening making the illustrations.

As class time came to an end they were still asking each other questions, trying to predict the type of questions that might be asked. In the end they agreed to get to school an hour early the next morning to meet and discuss any other possible concerns.

Group Four, consisting of Terry Somilleda, Sylvia Casillas, Danny Velasquez, and Phoung Tran, came into class on Friday well prepared to present the Silly Circle Value Theorem, which became known as the SCVT. (Note: the initials stand for the students' surnames as well as the title of the theorem.) Each of the team members had been assigned a part of the presentation.

Terry had spent the evening drawing simple, extremely accurate illustrations on three separate pieces of poster board for the presentation. Sylvia, the creator of the title of the discovery, made the clear, valid presentation of the logical arguments supporting their idea. And their plan was for Danny (who always was questioning everything) and Phoung to answer all questions from the class. They had divided up the labor equitably, but during the class it wasn't quite as organized as they had hoped.

Danny and Phoung held up Terry's pictures, and as Sylvia tried to explain things, Terry couldn't help interrupting with further explanations for her illustrations. Sylvia was nervous, and evidently Phoung had memorized the entire presentation because wherever Sylvia slipped up Phoung corrected her. And before the conclusion Danny was involved in the explanation of the discovery. Danny and Phoung had a vested interest in the validity of the presentation because the more logical the proof, the fewer the questions.

During the questions all of the group responded, not just Phoung and Danny. Due to the title they had given the discovery and the way it involved their initials, the group had a special reason for this presentation to become part of their book. They owned it. So when the time came for the vote, all four of them were especially nervous. But they had done an excellent job and the vote was unanimous in favor of making the Silly Circle Value Theorem a part of their book. (Note: the SCVT describes the method for determining the number of degrees in an arc of a circle, and it appears in Appendix 3.)

Appendix 3

$\approx$

An Actual Build-A-Book Textbook

The following pages are a photo-reproduction of the cover and text of an actual, student-created Build-A-Book book. It was not developed in the first No Book class, but is the product of one semester's work from a later class. This particular book was included because it is both typical and unique—typical because it reflects the creative mathematics content found in the final books of each Build-A-Book experiment and unique because the class that created it was the only BAB class to have worked in a traditional geometry course the first semester. They became a BAB class the second semester due to a shortage of books. In this book, you'll find definitions, discoveries, dedications, explanations, and the kind of geometry that occurs in a BAB class. Students also included before and after quotes that reflect their attitudes. (And no, they didn't know you'd be reading it!)

PERIOD 3 BAB CHAPTERS
Final Edition

FORWARD

The 1990-91 SUNBURST/ Build-A-Book 3 period Geometry class has gone through dramatic changes! At the beginning of this school year we started with Sunburst, a geometry book written by authors who wanted us to accept everything that they wrote as true, which we did unquestioningly! We were doing mindless school work and boring homework. Deep down inside we really didn't care about what we were learning, only about our grades!

After a big argument at the end of the first semester, over whether or not to keep our book, we had a vote! This vote was to determine wether we wanted to keep on doing mindless work and boring homework or go on to a different style of learning, called BAB! The vote was in favor for the book (as we said earlier we were only interested in grades)! Our teacher, Mr Healy, on the other hand thought it would be fun to see what the out come would be, if our class became a BAB class. This was the first class he had taught that went from using a book to BAB, and we succeeded!

DEDICATION

This last edition of the 1991 BAB 3rd period geometry book is dedicated to Mr. Christopher C. Healy because of his persistence in giving us more responsibilities and freedom to run the class. Most of the times he would say he lost our investigation sheets or misplaced the agendum, also his child-like gift of never answering any of our questions with a straight answer, it drove some people to insanity (and was extremely annoying) but it helped to open our minds and let our ideas (as weird as they may seem) of what we thought geometry was, become reality.

He gave the students with little interest in the class support and confidence in education and made them feel intelligent. He also helped the smart, little know it alls deflate their egos and see other people as intelligent persons. But most of all he brought a new meaning to student responsibility and the student-teacher relationship (making us realize that they make many mistakes too).

To all these things we thank you Mr. Healy because if it wasn't for you we'd probably be buried in a regular geometry book accepting facts that don't make sense. We, the 3rd period BAB geometry class, would like to applaud for your actions, Mr. Healy,

THANK YOU!!!

INTRODUCTION

We, thirty people of 3rd period BAB would like to introduce to you our way of looking at Geometry! We have all taken different paths, at one time or the other, while building this book! For instance, while one group was involved with constructing ovals another group was heavily into trigonometry. But one thing we all had in common was we had to depend on each other's thoughts and ideas to keep moving forward! The reason we depended on each other so much was because we did not have a traditional teacher to depend on, to give us all the information.

It was a surprise to all that we did so well in our venture into BAB. We were all used to having a regular book and teacher, since we went through a whole semester of it already.

This is what the students thought about the book and BAB.

Before	After
In BAB we'd learn everything wrong and our grades would be even worse.	It has built up my self confidence. You go through a lot of changes in BAB I have become more involved in class, in all my classes in fact.
I don't want to go into a BAB because my grade will be lowered and it will ruin my GPA. I need the security of a book.	I'm no longer afraid to speak up. I now prefer BAB and don't care about my grade. For a class to change all my point of view is very rare. taking a BAB class is the one experience everyone should try in HS.

I don't like BAB, because I learned how to use a book ever since I was in school, I'm used to it.

I DO NOT want BAB because I am afraid my grades will drop. Besides am used to the old and I hate changing into something totally new.

I want to go to BAB. I think it would be a fun change. I got a "D" in this class and I want to try something new.

I don't want a BAB class. It will hurt my grades and my parents don't allow less than a"B". I won't learn the geometry all the other classes know. If they ask me a question I would answer," I don't take geometry."

My friends tell me the BAB tests are pure trick questions. I wouldn't mind having BAB if it was easier to get a good grade.

I want BAB, something different. I'm failing anyway.

I desire to have an "A" in this class. I learned a lot from BAB. It changed my learning method.

I found out I can do anything, if I put my mind to it. Starting this class was pretty risky. I am proud of myself for taking that risk.

I take things more seriously now. I talk about geometry in class, but also outside and at home (all over the place). I would do BAB all over again.

All my friends and parents think I am not the same person. Before I never said anything, even if I didn't agree. Not any more now I talk back and tell them what I think its right. I feel proud and I will tell everyone that I have been through BAB.

BAB made grades less important to me. Made me involved in everything, increased my self confidence, helped me believe in myself. I'm glad I was in a BAB class.

I'm learning to speak in front of the class. Every math class should experience both BAB and using a text.

I want a book to study on the day of the test.
P.S. Please give us BOOK FOR GEOMETRY!?!!

No BAB, because we wouldn't have any source of information to fall ack on if we need help. We can't trust our own judgement, not knowing if we are right. We won't be learning geometry. Those people who are failing like me may find it more difficult.

#1 With a book students learn facts and can check their answers in the book.
#2 In your geometry classes you don't teach anything. BAB can't even check if they have the right answers. They make up their own facts which are probably mostly WRONG!
My biggest fears
1) my grades!
2) I WON'T LEARN geometry.

I can present in front of the without being embarrassed. I hated working with computers and now I need a computer beside me. My feeling towards BAB is fun and success. Even though I failed this class, I experienced being a member of BAB. I'm going to take geometry next year and I know I'll pass it.

BAB has taught me to depend on myself. I don't need someone to show the way. I gained self-confidence. At first it was confusing and hard. It taught me I can be myself. I believe I can get things done the right way and not think someone is going to put me down.

Grades don't worry me as much anymore. I learned how to stand up in front of a crowd without being afraid. I learned to question things. I even question my parents and stand up to them when I know I am right. I learned how to prove things to them. When I was up in front I prove to the class "Hey, I'm not as dumb as I look, you know!" Mr. Healy, you should let all of your students have a textbook and do BAB, it will really benefit them.

TABLE OF CONTENTS

The 1991 Build a Book class consisted of the following people:

Lily Alvarez	Brian Maco
Omero Banuelos	Sergio Medina
Silvia Casillas	Maria Mendez
Cyndi Castro	Quynh-Anh Nguyen
Amanda Chavez	Binh Pham
Richard Dominguez	Tran Phung
Nubia Escamilla	Gabby Quiroz
Rene Flores	Erica Raygoza
Bernadette Hernandez	Terry Somilleda
Ivette Hernandez	Debbie To
Andy Ho	Peter Tran
Maggie Ho	Phuong Tran
Jesus Huerta	Danny Velasquez
Tram Huynh	Patrick Vengua
Jenny Lai	Hector Verdugo

PHYSICAL AND IMAGINARY GEOMETRY

There are two types of geometry, as you read through this book keep these ideas and thoughts in mind because geometry is different for every individual.

Imaginary geometry starts with an answer and ends with a question. Imaginary geometry goes beyond what you see on paper to what you see in your mind. Imaginary geometry is a way to look at physical geometry. Physical geometry is what you're taught and imaginary geometry is what you think and "imagine". Physical geometry has limits and imaginary geometry has no rules or boundaries. Imaginary geometry is different for every individual.

Physical geometry is a kind of step towards imaginary geometry, you need to know a little physical geometry then your mind can take it from there. In physical geometry when you get stuck on a problem you stop and go to imaginary geometry so that you feel you're not stuck any more and can make-up an answer.

Chapter 1
Lines

Definitions:

curved line- a mark that is not straight.

parallel lines- Two lines extending in the same direction at a constant distance apart that never meet. Two straight lines that lie on the same plane no matter how far they extend.

perpendicular bisector- the line passing through the midpoint of AB and perpendicular to AB. For every point P on the perpendicular bisector PA = PB.

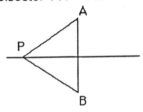

perpendicular lines -Two straight lines which intersect to form 90 degree angles.

midpoint of a line segment divides a line segment into two equal parts.

ray- A straight line extending from an endpoint.
        (A ray has only 1 endpoint)

straight line- a one dimensional straight mark.

Important Ideas

Each point on the perpendicular bisector of a line segment is equidistant from the endpoints of the line segment.

PARALLEL POSTULATE - Given any line *m* and a point P not on *m*, there is one and only one line through P parallel to *m* .

If a point is equidistant from the endpoint of a line segment, then it is on the perpendicular bisector of the segment.

If line *l* and *m* are parallel lines, then any two line segments drawn from the endpoints on *l* and *m* respectively, and perpendicular to both *l* and *m*, have the same length.

THE REFLECTION OF A POINT ACROSS A LINE - If *l* is a line and B a point not on *l*, then the reflection of B* such that:
(i) the distance from B* to *l* is equal to the distance from B to *l*, and
(ii) the line joining B to B* is perpendicular to *l*.

Chapter 2-Angles

Definitions

acute angle- an angle less than 90 degrees.

angle-Two rays or lines that intersect each other at a common point   (measured in degrees).

axiom- a statement which is accepted as true, without proof.

base angles of an Isosceles triangle are the angles opposite the sides of equal length.

bisector of an angle is a ray through the vertex of an angle.

obtuse angle- an angle greater than 90 degrees.

right angle- an angle equal to 90 degrees.

straight angle- An angle having 180 degrees.

theorem - a statement that can be proved using previously established or accepted facts.

vertex- The point of intersection of any 2 sides, lines, or rays.

Important Ideas

Vertical angles are equal.

The sum of the acute angles of a right triangle is 90 degrees.

vertex of an angle, **sides** of an angle.

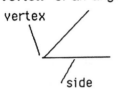

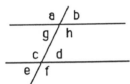

The two horizontal lines are parallel in order to have the following (the following are examples):

<g and <b are vertical angles
<b and <d are corresponding angles
<c and <h are alternate interior angles

Chapter 3- Triangles

Given Info.

In any right triangle a squared plus b squared equals c squared.

Definitions

altitude of a triangle is a line segment drawn from a vertex perpendicular to the opposite side.

equilateral triangle- a regular 3-gon; a **square** is a regular 4-gon.

hypotenuse of a right triangle is the side opposite the right angle. The other two sides are called the **legs.**

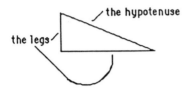

isosceles triangle is a triangle having two or more sides of equal length.

median of a triangle is a line segment joining a vertex to the midpoint of the opposite side.

right triangle- a triangle having a right angle.

Important Ideas

TRIANGLE INEQUALITY - The length of any side of a triangle is less than the sum of the lengths of the other two sides.

EXTERIOR ANGLE THEOREM -Any exterior angle of a triangle is equal to the sum of the opposite interior angles.

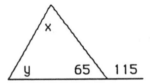

Any exterior angle of a triangle is equal to the sum of the opposite interior angles because:
1. A straight angle has 180 degrees in which 65+115=180 degrees.
2. A triangle also has 180 degrees in which x+y+65=180 degrees.
3. Therefore, the sum of the opposite interior angles which are x+y must equal 115 degrees in order for it to be 180 degrees if added to the 65 degree angle.

The line segment joining the midpoint of two sides of a triangle is parallel to the third side and has half the length of the third side.

The sum of the angles of any triangle is 180 degrees.

The SSS property of triangles

The SAS property of triangles

The ASA property of triangles

Corresponding parts of congruent triangles are equal.

Conversely, if two angles of a triangle are equal, then the triangle is an isosceles (the sides opposite the equal angles have equal length).

In any **30-60 degree** right triangle, the side opposite the 30 degree angle has a length **half** of the hypotenuse.

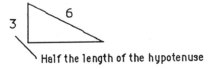

Half the length of the hypotenuse

The length of the hypotenuse of an isosceles right triangle with legs of length a is a with the square root of 2.

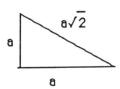

The angle bisectors of a triangle all meet in a point.

The extended altitudes of a triangle meet in a point.

The medians of a triangle meet in a point.

Chapter 4- Figures

Given Info.

Figures can have the same shape, but different size.

Definitions

degree congruent- Figures that have the same sum of degrees.

figure-The outer form of any geometric object.

inner congruent- The inside of figures are congruent.

mass congruent-Figures being congruent in area or volume.

n-gon- A polygon with *n* sides.

outer congruent- Congruent in only the outside parts of figures.

parallelogram- A quadrilateral whose opposite sides are parallel and equal.

proportional-Corresponding in size, degree and shape.

proportional figures-Figures that correspond in size,degree and shape.

quadrilateral-A four sided figure.

rectangle- A parallelogram whose angles are all 90 degrees.

regular polygon- An n-gon all of whose angles are equal and all whose sides have equal length.

resemble-to have similarity or likeness. To be or look alike [not exactly alike].

shape- A figure.

side-A straight line or surface forming a border or face of a solid figure.

symmetric-Opposite parts of a figure being equal in size, shape, and position.

Important Ideas

Each interior angle of a regular n-gon is $\dfrac{(n-2)(180 \text{ degrees})}{n}$

The sum of the angles of any n-gon is (n-2)(180 degrees)

Any parallelogram has the following properties:
> A diagonal cuts it into two congruent triangles.
> Opposite sides have equal length and are parallel.
> The diagonals bisect each other.

A quadrilateral is a parallelogram if it has any of the following properties:
> Each pair of opposite sides are of equal length.
> Two of its sides are parallel and of equal length.
> Its diagonals bisect each other.

The diagonals of a rectangle have the same length.

If the diagonals of a parallelogram have the same length, then it is a rectangle.

Chapter 5- Circles and Constructions

Given Info.

A circle has 360 degrees.

Definitions

An **arc** of a circle is a part of a circle lying between two points on the circumference of the circle.

A **chord** of a circle is a line segment joining two points on the circumference of the circle.

A **diameter** of a circle is a chord passing though the center of the circle.

oval- A symmetrical circle that is stretched from opposite arcs having 360 degrees with no angles.

Important Ideas

A **circle** of radius *r* with center *p* consists of all those points in the plane that are at distance *r* from *p*.

The perpendicular bisector of any chord of a circle passes through the center of that circle.

Constructions:

To construct an oval- First, draw 2 circles that are intersected. Find the center of the 1st circle and the point at the top where the circles intersect. Use a compass to measure both points, then mark an arc at the top of the circumference of the 1st circle. Now find the point at the bottom where the two circles intersect, measuring from that point to the arc , then make another arc until it extends and touches the 2nd circle.

Do the same thing to the bottom by measuring the point at the bottom and the center of the 1st circle. Mark an arc at the bottom of the circumference of the 1st circle. Then find the point at the top where the two circles intersect, measure that point and the arc at the bottom, then make and arc extended to the second circle exactly like the top, but this time do it at the bottom.

Steps in drawing an oval

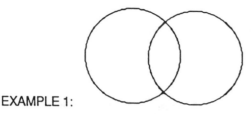

EXAMPLE 1:

EXAMPLE 2:   EXAMPLE 3:

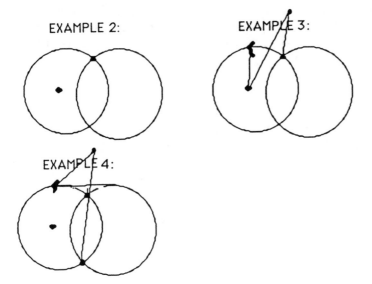

EXAMPLE 4:

Project Oval
Constructing an oval with 2 distant (non-connecting) circles

Steps in drawing the oval...

1st-draw 2 non-intersecting circles with any equal   radius, and any distance between them. Label center points B and T.

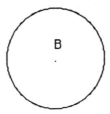

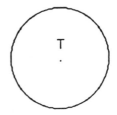

2nd-measure the distance between point B &T with a compass, draw a line connecting both points. With the same compass setting draw a perpendicular bisector of BT with endpoints ED. Find the outer points A and C that are on the line segment BT.

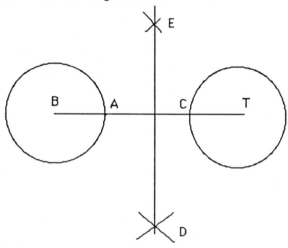

3rd-measure the distance between B & A, then make a mark on the circumference of the circle with center point B. Using the same compass setting, mark another arc on the radius of the circle, and label this point F.

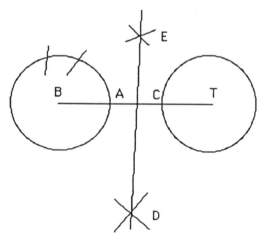

4th-measuring from point D to point F, make an arc extending until it touches circle T.

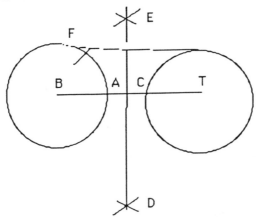

5th-Do the exact same thing to the other side of both circles.

Chapter 6- Areas and Volume

Important Ideas

The fundamental properties of area (the following are examples):
I.   The area of a rectangle with base *b* and height *h* is *bh*.
II. If two figures are congruent, then they have the same area.
III. If a figure is cut into pieces, then the area of the figure is the sum of
     the area of the pieces.

The fundamental properties of volume (the following are examples):
I.   The volume of a rectangular box with edges *a, b,* and *c* is *abc*.
II. If two solids are congruent, then they have the same volume.
III. If a solid is cut into pieces, then the volume of the solid is the sum of the volumes of the pieces.

Any **parallelogram** with base *b* and altitude *h* has area equal to *bh*.

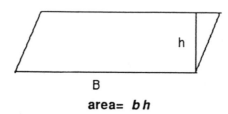

B

area= *bh*

Any **triangle** with base *b* and altitude *h* has area equal to $\frac{1}{2}bh$

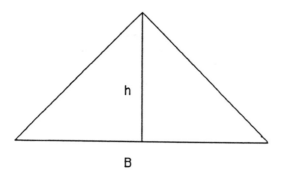

h

B

area= $\frac{1}{2}bh$

Any **trapezoid** of height *h* and parallel sides of length *a* and *b* respectively has area equal to $\frac{1}{2}h\,(a+b)$

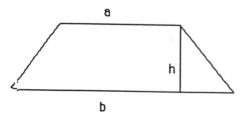

a

h

b

Area= $\frac{1}{2}h\,(a+b)$

Any **prism** with height h and base area A has volume equal to h A.
V= h A

Any **pyramid** with altitude h and base area A has volume equal to $\frac{1}{3}$ h A

$$V = \frac{1}{3} h \text{ A}$$

Chapter 7- Explanations and Theorems

Explanation #1

Corresponding angles are equal if the lines are parallel:

Explanation: In order for corresponding angles to be equal, lines l and m must be parallel. If the lines l and m are not parallel they will eventually intersect forming a triangle and causing the difference of degrees in the corresponding angles. **For example:**

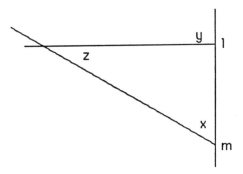

1. Y=X+Z   1. Because of the exterior
            angle theorem.

2. Y>X   2. Because Y is greater than X
            as proved in *1.

Explanation #2

The sum of each angle in a regular n-gon is [n-2(180)]

Choose a vertex on an n-gon , Draw the diagonals from this point to all of the other vertices on the regular n-gon. The resulting is 2 triangles less than the amount of sides.

Ex: in a five-gon, there will be 3 triangles after the diagonals are drawn. In a regular eight-gon, there will be 6 complete triangles.

each triangle has 180 degrees, therefore, the sum of the angles in each n-gon is equal to (n-2)(180).

To find the sum of each angle just divide by n

Explanation #3

The formula of (n-2) (180 degrees)- We know it's true because if we have a 6-gon and choose a vertex. Call it A. Draw the diagonals from A to each vertex the three diagonals will form four triangles. Since each triangle is 180 degrees. 180 degrees x 4 triangles = 720 degrees.

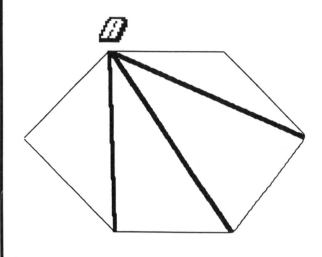

Explanation # 5

Diagonals of a rectangle are equal.

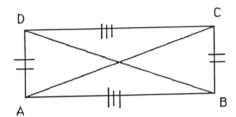

they are equal because of the following proof:

STATEMENT	REASON
1. DA=CB	1. Opposite sides of a rectangle are parallel and equal.
2. <A=<B	2. Both are 90 degrees because all angles of a rectangle are 90 degrees.
3. AB=AB	3. Anything equals itself.
4. △DAB = △CBA	4. SAS
5. DB = AC	5. CP of congruent triangles are equal.

Explanation # 6

Any △ with base "B" and height "H" has an area 1/2 of BH

The area of the rectangle is bh, the diagonal of a rectangle divides the rectangle into two congruent △'s. One △ is half of the rectangle. Therefore the area of one of the △'s must be half bh, in other words half the area of the rectangle. Example:

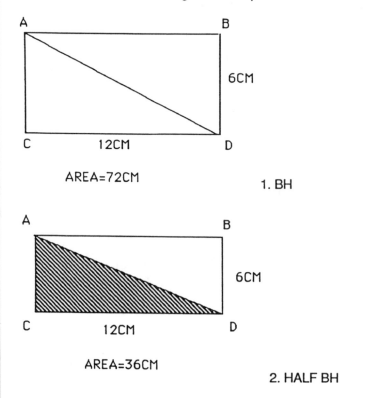

AREA=72CM

1. BH

AREA=36CM

2. HALF BH

Explanation # 7

The sum of the acute angles in a right△ is 90 degrees

The sum of all the angles in a triangle equals 180 degrees. In a right triangle there is a 90 degree angle. So the sum of the other two angles has to be 90 degrees in order to form a right triangle.

Explanation #8
In any right triangle the line segment joining the vertex of the right angle to the midpoint of the hypotenuse is half the length of the hypotenuse. Since the diagonals of a rectangle are equal and since the diagonals bisect at one point, point E, (as the picture shows) point E is the midpoint of the hypotenuse. Therefore the line segment will pass through point E in to another imaginary congruent triangle.

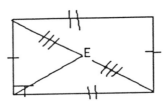

Explanation #9

ASA (angle, side, angle)

If the two triangles have the same angles and sides congruent, there would be two sides that are not yet drawn. Extended segment from the angles would both meet in a common point. Those two sides would be congruent to the second triangle's two sides.

SAS (SIDE, ANGLE, SIDE)

SAS (SIDE, ANGLE, SIDE) - Two or more triangles that are congruent by a   side and an angle and a side in that order.
Sides AC is equal to BD because opposite sides of a rectangle is equal. Sides AB is equal to CD because opposite sides of a rectangle is equal. <A=<D because the rectangle has 90 degrees. Therefore the two triangles are congruent by SAS.

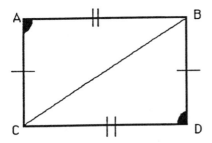

SSS (SIDE, SIDE, SIDE) - Two or more triangle are congruent in all three sides.
AB=DC because opposite sides of a rectangle is equal. AD=BC because of the same reason. AC=AC because anything equals itself. Therefore the two triangles are congruent by SSS.

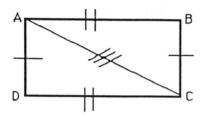

Explanation #10

The area of any parallelogram with base "B" and height "H" is BH

1. Divide the parallelogram into 2 equal triangles by drawing a diagonal of the parallelogram.

2. Figure the area of the triangle by using half bh.

3. Then add the areas of two triangles.

4. The sum of the areas of the two triangles is equal to the area of the whole parallelogram.

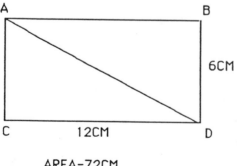

AREA=72CM

1. BH

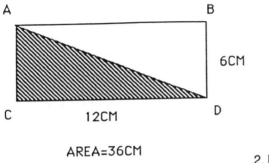

AREA=36CM

2. HALF BH

Explanation #11

MOUNT CYNDI

If side B is 45 feet and angle 1 is 15 degrees, so if we use the formula : tangent= A/B .
.2679 =A/45 feet
A=(45 feet)(.2679)
A= 12.0555

B=45 feet

Each angle has a different tangent depending on the degree of angle 1.

ANGLE	TANGENT
5 dg.	.0875
10 dg.	.1763
15 dg.	.2679
20 dg.	.3640
25 dg.	.4663
30 dg.	.5774
35 dg.	.7002
40 dg.	.8391
45 dg.	1.000
50 dg.	1.192
55 dg.	1.428
60 dg.	1.732
65 dg.	2.145
70 dg.	2.747
75 dg.	3.732
80 dg.	5.671
85 dg.	11.43

Explanation #12

Connecting the midpoints of the sides of any quadrilateral makes a parallelogram.
1. Diagonal **AC** divides quadrilateral **ABCD** into 2 triangles.
2. **EF= and parallel to GH** because connecting the midpoints of 2 sides of a triangle is equal to **1/2 of AC** and parallel to the third side which is **AC.**

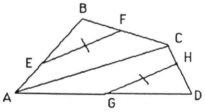

3. Diagonal **BD** divides quadrilateral **ABCD** into 2 triangles.
4. **EG = and parallel to FH;** same as #2.

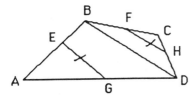

5. Therefore, connecting the midpoints of a quadrilateral makes a parallelogram because opposite sides **EG and FH** is parallel and equal to each other. The same goes for **EF and GH**.

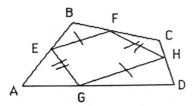

Explanation #13

A circle has tiny straight sides and lots of big angles. When we draw a circle using a compass we form no angles and no straight lines. The circle is made up of curved lines, a curved line is not straight: with curved lines, there is no existing angles unless the circle is divided. Compass drawing:

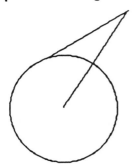

The computer is not accurate with its drawings.
Computer fat bits:

Theorems

AHQN triangle theorem- A triangle has 180 degrees. To prove this, a triangle is form within 2 parallel lines by 2 lines that cross the parallel lines.

<3+<4+<5= 180 degrees because a straight angle has 180 degrees. <2=<4 because alternate interior angles are equal. The same goes with <1 and <3. <5=<5 because anything will equal itself. Therefore, <1+<2+<5= 180 degrees.
(look at picture)

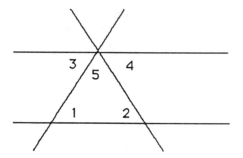

Silly Circle Value Theorem (SCVT)

Measuring Arcs

SCVT A. To measure an arc you must find the center of the circle that the arc is part of. To find the center of a circle, we draw 2 sets of 2 points on the circumference of the circle. Then you connect the points to form 2 chords. You bisect each chord and extend that line towards the middle of the circle where they will both meet on a point. That will be the center of the circle.

SCVT B. Afterwards you connect the endpoints of your first arc, to the center of your circle. Measure the arc, like an angle, and this will give you the degrees of the arc.

NUDE Theorem

The **NUDE theorem** states that the center angle is 2x the outer angle.
We think that the **NUDE theorem** definitely works to find the degrees of the outer angle when the center angle is given (and vice-versa).

How to do this:

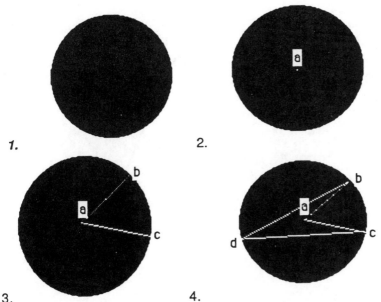

1.

2.

3.   4.

1.Draw any circle. Find the center point A. Find any two points B and C, on the circle and connect to the center point A. This forms the center angle. Next find any point D on the circle that would form an acute angle. Connect B and C to D. This forms the outer angle.
The formula to follow is: angle y = 1/2 angle x.
The Nude Theorem works if the following properties are in effect:
2.The center angle must be 180 angles or less.
3. The outer angle must be an acute angle.

MAG-DEB THEOREM

Connecting the midpoint of an uneven arrow makes a parallelogram or a rectangle.
1) Draw an uneven arrow.
2) Find the midpoint of the segment. ex. AC, AB
.3) Connect the midpoints.
The connection of the midpoints forms a parallelogram or

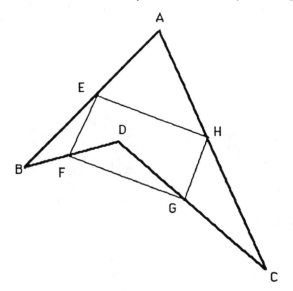

rectangle.

SERGE'S THEOREM

A=BH for a Parallelogram
This is true, because if you tile the parallelogram, the number of base squares multiply by the number of height squares would be equal to the total number of squares : Therefore A=BH
Example:

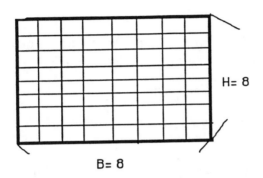

H= 8

B= 8

BXH=A, 8X8=64   64 total number of squares

APPENDIX

Response to the question: How has BAB changed you?

I am free to express myself now. I used to be very, very shy.

It made me work.

When I come into class I have to think about what we are going to do and I don't just sit there anymore.

I take things more serious now. I not only talk about geometry in class, but outside and at home (and all over the place).

I feel more confident about my tests.

I speak up now. Sometimes it gets me into trouble. I'll say something I shouldn't have, but wanted to, and "Bam, I'm busted."

It taught me how to work well with people in my group.

I can do anything if I just put my mind to it.

It changed the way I look towards my classmates. I used to think that they weren't very intelligent, but I learned that even if they don't get good grades that they are more intelligent than me. It made me learn to cooperate.

My public speaking has really improved.

I learned to stand up in front of a crowd without being afraid. And I learned to question things. I even question my parents and stand up for myself when I know I'm right.

I learned to depend on myself. I don't need one to lead the way.

I can now present in front of the class without being embarrassed I usually hate working with computers, but now on every investigation I need a computer by my side.

BAB gave me a chance to think about something that seemed complicated and to express my feelings.

It made talking to my Dad about geometry a lot easier. It's fun, because I understand it.

I can disagree when I feel things are wrong.

I became more involved in BAB (and also in my other classes). It has also made me question the significance of many things.

BAB requires more effort from you than other classes.

To speak my mind and talk in front.

I have confidence in myself now.

Gave me courage to give my opinion. It helped me not to be afraid of public speaking. I want to be involved in everything now. The class helped my self confidence.

I feel secure in this class. I learned to speak out loud.

Now I ask questions and participate and don't worry my grade.

I think of my grade more. I haven't changed, my parents have. They tell me to work harder.

Turned me into a curious monster. In my other classes I try to find out why things happen now.

In BAB I don't have to follow any rules.

When I came into this class if there was a problem I couldn't do I just gave up, but now I find ways to make it work.

All of my friends and my parents tell me I'm not me anymore. Before I used to be a little wimp. Before I accepted what people told me, but now I talk back and tell them what I think is right.

INDEX

AFTERWORD

This BAB class changed many of the students who participated in it. This changed was a different kind of change. It was not only in the way we looked toward geometry, but also in the way we looked toward ourselves and others.

The experiences we went through in this BAB class gave most of us confidence in ourselves and in our abilities. Arguing, during class, with our classmates greatly improved our abilities in expressing ourselves in our own unique ways.

BAB also brought out a lot of effort from us. We had to think logically and reasonably in order to prove, to our classmates, that our point of views were right. There were no rules or limitations on what we did in our class. We only accepted things into our book that had reasonable explanations backing them up. Therefore, the 1991 3rd period BAB class was definitely unique in the way that we had a chance to express ourselves and learn from our peers.

About the Cover

The front cover art for *Build-A-Book Geometry* is by Bernie Garcia, a former No Book Geometry student who makes a cameo appearance in this book. Bernie is now a Sophomore studying art and design at California Polytechnical State University in San Luis Obispo, California.